ROOF AND TERRACE GARDENS

WITHDRAWN

Published in Great Britain in 2008
by John Wiley & Sons Ltd

Other Wiley Editorial Offices

John Wiley & Sons Inc., 111 River Street, Hoboken,
NJ 07030, USA

Jossey-Bass, 989 Market Street, San Francisco,
CA 94103-1741, USA

Wiley-VCH Verlag GmbH, Boschstr. 12,
D-69469 Weinheim, Germany

John Wiley & Sons Australia Ltd, 42 McDougall Street,
Milton, Queensland 4064, Australia

John Wiley & Sons (Asia) Pte Ltd, 2 Clementi Loop #02-01,
Jin Xing Distripark, Singapore 129809

John Wiley & Sons Canada Ltd, 5353 Dundas Street West,
Suite 400, Etobicoke, Ontario M9B 6H8, Canada

Wiley also publishes its books in a variety of electronic
formats. Some content that appears in print may not be
available in electronic books.

Executive Commissioning Editor: Helen Castle
Project Editor: Miriam Swift
Publishing Assistant: Calver Lezama

ISBN 978-0-470-51761-1

Cover photo © Steve Gorton

Cover design © Jeremy Tilston, The Oak Studio Limited

Photo credits
All photographs by Steve Gorton unless stated below:
p 8: © Urbis Design, pp 10, 76: © Urban Roof Gardens Ltd,
pp 19, 26, 45: © The Garden Trellis Company Ltd,
pp 34, 67: © David Harber Ltd,
pp 84, 86, 87, 89, 90, 91: © Blackdown Horticultural
Consultants Ltd

Page design and layouts by
Jeremy Tilston, The Oak Studio Limited
Prepress by Artmedia Press Ltd • London
Printed and bound by Printer Trento, Italy

ROOFTOP AND TERRACE GARDENS

Garden Style Guides

CAROLINE TILSTON

Photography by Steve Gorton

ROOFTOP AND TERRACE GARDENS

INFORMATION

INSPIRATION

Introduction

Gardening on high is a matter of extremes – the sun is hotter, the wind is stronger, the prices higher, the seclusion and excitement amazing.

One of the most extreme things about creating or updating a roof or terrace garden, which is pretty much common to every case, is the lack of soil beneath your feet. You are making a garden in an environment that has no natural plants or trees, everything will have to be brought in – and you are in control. Talk about a blank canvas!

And that's the way it is with roof and terrace gardens. What might be seen as a restriction (not having any soil is going to scupper lots of plans), can be turned into a great benefit if you work with it and think in terms of containers, minimalism, structural planting.

So it's worth looking at the restrictions and benefits of roof gardens in general and thinking about how they apply to your space in particular before you do anything else.

This architectural plant design is set off by the modern planter from Urbis Design.

Benefits of a roof or terrace garden

Creates another room Making the most of a terrace or roof will effectively make another room or at least add more usable space to your home.

Adds value to a property Making another room will increase the value of your property.

Environmental benefits Every time you put a plant on a roof you are helping the environment in lots of ways – any greenery is welcome in cities.

Makes the most of any great views Hopefully you will get some amazing views from up above – even a view across other rooftops can be enchanting.

Privacy The garden is less likely to be overlooked than one at ground level.

Freedom to express yourself That privacy also means you are less likely to have visual references for the garden. You can do what you like with the design of the space and not worry about it clashing with what is around it.

Sun It will probably be very sunny and light and unlikely to have the deep shadows of a garden at ground level.

Low maintenance Because there's no soil there naturally, it's easy to have fewer plants – and that means lower maintenance. So, if you want to, you get the fresh air and a lovely place to sit without any of the hassle of a garden.

Disadvantages and difficulties of creating a roof or terrace garden

Practical restrictions Weight, access etc. I've devoted a whole chapter of this book to these points as it's important to get these absolutely right, but don't be put off. Apart from anything else (like the enjoyment you will get from it), the garden is likely to be a sound investment.

Wind Above ground level the wind tends to be stronger and you need to be careful to make sure nothing can blow off. Also, make sure there are sheltered places to sit out of the wind.

Watering All that wind and sun and lack of soil will mean any plants you do have will dry out quickly and need a lot of additional watering. An automatic system will probably be a good idea if you're having anything other than extremely minimal planting.

No soil This can be an advantage if you don't want plants and don't like gardening, but if you do want some plants the soil or compost will have to be brought to the site and its weight will have to be accommodated on the roof.

Tend to be small Again, if all you want to do is sit in the sun, small can be beautiful, but if you have ideas of rolling acres, it's just not going to happen on a roof.

Making a terrace or roof garden

There is a real growing movement to make the most of roofs and terraces – for environmental reasons, and to make the most of every last inch of available space in, on or around the home.

Sarah Bevin from Urban Roof Gardens, a company specialising in creating gardens in the sky, answers some questions that will help get you started …

This London garden by Urban Roof Gardens takes on a new feel at night when the lights in the garden match the excitement of the city around.

Q&A

Can I make a terrace or roof garden?

Three things you will need – if you don't have these it's a non-starter.

- Space outside that belongs to you and you are allowed to use. (Check the deeds of your property.)
- The space needs to be load bearing or can be reinforced to be load bearing.
- You will need to have access to the space – possibly through a door or window.

Can I have a roof garden if my roof is pitched?

It's easier to make a usable space if the roof is flat but even if you have a pitched roof it's not impossible to make a garden outside. One way is to cut into the roof to make a flat space – a kind of inverted dormer.

What else might stop me having a terrace or roof garden?

Planning and building regulations. Always ask your local planning department before you start. The Royal Town Planning Institute says roof gardens usually require planning consent if they overlook other properties or if the creation of the terrace includes the building of substantial walls or major work such as installing an additional staircase; there may also be other issues specific to your space, so it's always best to check.

Anything else?

Privacy issues often dictate the amount of space you can make usable and the planning may stipulate screening.

What if there's a window to the space but no door?

A window opening out onto a terrace can be changed into a door by making use of the existing structural opening – so no new lintels.

What if there's a ladder to the roof but no proper staircase? Should I put in a spiral staircase?

A proper staircase will take up more room both inside the house and on the roof than the ladder but easier access may be a priority for you. A spiral staircase actually takes up more ground space than a conventional staircase and can be more difficult to negotiate.

How much will it cost?

You know what I'm going to say … it all depends. The more structural work that needs doing, the more the basic cost will be. Structural work includes things like putting in barriers, reinforcing the roof, and once that's done, it's possible to spend an awful lot on furniture, lighting and accessories if you want to. But remember that creating a whole new, usable area for a house will add to its value.

Where's the best place to start?

Look at this book, obviously, but also I would ask an architect with experience in roof gardens to have a look and give you an idea of the feasibility of what you have in mind. Specialist firms such as the Urban Roof Gardens team include architects and structural engineers with huge experience in this area.

How do you begin the design of the terrace or roof garden?

One thing we ask: do you want the space connected completely to the house because it is an outside room and visually linked to the house, or do you go for the unexpected? Away from ground level you may feel freer to express yourself, so the design can be liberated from restrictions. Also ask yourself what you want from the roof or terrace and how you will use it. Questions like: will you go out or just view it? Do you want wildlife and greenery or a smart outdoor room?

Can I have a proper garden with plants and trees?

Usually planting is in containers or raised beds and these can be big enough to contain trees, the main restriction will be on weight. Planting can also be grown directly onto the roof using a lightweight growing medium – this is common in 'green roofs' (see Chapter 10).

This book

Part I
Information

There's a very logical way to design and lay out any garden, a sequence to go through to get to the garden that you want and which will suit the space. Overall the process is the same for any garden and it goes like this …

1. Gather information about the site.
2. Gather information about what you want from the site.
3. Get inspiration for the design
4. Put the design together – make the spaces.
5. Decide how to form those spaces with vertical and horizontal elements.
6. Add decorative elements and planting.

However, there is a difference with roof and terrace gardens, the information you gather about the site needs to be very specific and detailed. What's beneath your feet cannot be taken for granted – it's not solid earth. Nowhere, in any other part of garden-making, is the technology of the structure more interdependent with the design.

CHAPTER 1: Is your roof ready for a garden?

So, where normally I'd try to start with something positive and inspirational, I've started this book with the practicalities. These so dominate the design, the planting, everything about roof and terrace gardens, it's worth putting them front and centre in the book.

CHAPTER 2: Gathering information

This goes through the 'normal' process of design – gathering information about the garden and about what you want from it.

CHAPTER 3: Creating spaces

This brings all of this information together to start creating spaces within the garden – creating the design.

CHAPTER 4: Walls and floors

This goes through the options of how these rooms might be created – how the walls and the floors of the new space are made.

CHAPTER 5: Containers

Most planting on terraces and roofs will be in containers and they can also form a major part of the design so I've put in a whole chapter on how to design with them and how to plant them up.

CHAPTER 6: Water features

To find a water feature on a roof garden goes against expectations and that makes putting one in all the more exciting.

CHAPTER 7: Sculpture

Sculpture can really come into its own on a roof. When planting will probably be limited, art can add to the atmosphere and mood of the garden.

CHAPTER 8: Lighting

This is especially important if you can see the garden from inside the house. After dark it will be wonderful to replace that daytime view with an equally spectacular night-time one.

CHAPTER 9: Plants

Roof and terrace gardens present special environments for plants. Here's a directory of those that can cope, and look great.

CHAPTER 10: Green roofs

Green roofs are a special type of roof garden, designed mainly for the plants and the environment rather than for people to use; they are suited to roofs that are too small or structurally not able to take people.

Is your roof ready for a garden?

Roof gardens are much more constrained and led by practical and technical matters than any other type of garden. The design is completely interdependent with the technical issues – from the load-bearing abilities of the roof to the water runoff.

Whether you are starting from scratch or updating an existing garden it's worth going through the checklist – mistakes on roof gardens can be costly!

The first three are absolutely essential – if you think you have space that can be used or you want to change the design of a roof garden there are three things you really need to do …

Structural engineer/architect

Get someone who's experienced and qualified to look at the space and assess whether it's feasible to make a garden or update an existing one. If it is possible you will need a structural engineer to calculate the load-bearing capabilities of the roof in relation to what you want
to do.

Planning permission

Always check about this, it's worth a phone call to take advice on whether you need permission. If you are doing major works with walls and access routes you will almost certainly need it.

Building regulations

Again it always pays to check about these – regulators are particularly interested in loads, water runoff and making sure the building stays waterproof.

Whatever you do on the roof think about ...

- Safety
- Weight
- Waterproofing

Then there is a long list of other practical things to think about which will impact on the design ...

Issue	Possible impact on design
Will people be able to go on it or not? It sounds like an obvious question – but the garden may be too small or not able to take the weight of people moving around.	Even if you can't get out there you may still be able to make something beautiful to be enjoyed from the house – and lit at night. It means the view from the house will be the most important design element.
Access – for the build If you are going to put structures, plants, furniture up on the roof, think about how you're going to get the materials up there. Even bags of pebbles for a little pond can be a complete pain if you don't have a lift or if there are restrictions on what you can use the lift for.	Things like wood may need to be sawn up and put back together again – it's easier to make the design accommodate the maximum length of wood you can get up the stairs or in the lift. If you're really set on having something huge you could investigate using a crane.
Access – for use How are you going to get out or up to the roof every time you want to use it?	The easiest solution is a doorway at the same level as the roof, but if there's only a ladder, think about turning this into a stairway. It will be costly and take up room both on the roof and inside the building.

Fire escapes

If the roof is part of a fire escape make sure the exit way is kept clear.

Waterproofing

It's important not to damage the waterproofing membrane.

Protection from crime

Flat roofs are a point of entry for criminals and it's worth making sure that the doors are secure and anything left out on the roof is also secure.

Window cleaning?

Do you need to clean the windows – and how will this be done? It's a small point but if you make it really difficult to reach the glass it will be an annoyance.

You may need to mark access routes across the roof onto any design you do and keep them free.

Anything you would normally secure into the ground will have to be thought about carefully. The uprights of a pergola or fence, even little things like lights on spikes which can puncture the membrane.

Think about security lighting, extending the house alarm to the roof and its entry points. Contact your local crime prevention officer for further advice.

Probably putting the roof garden in will make access easier – but not if you put a flower bed right next to a window, or hang things off the building where the window cleaner needs to go.

Water runoff

Even a 'flat' roof will have a slight slope to take water away to drains or downpipes. If there is standing water it's bad news – eventually it will get through to the building.

Whatever you do on the roof you have to maintain these escape channels for water. Keep the slight slopes and do not block the drains.

Wind

Roofs tend to be windier than ground level gardens; there is usually a prevailing wind. However, in a city the buildings can cause the wind to scurry about and come from all directions.

Possible implications for the design:
- You may want windbreaks, securely attached.
- You may need structures for shelter.
- Furniture and other objects may have to be heavy so they aren't blown around or off the roof.

A trellis like this (from the Garden Trellis Company) will slow the wind down and make your area more comfortable where a solid barrier would create more turbulence.

Cables and pipes

There may be loads of cables up there already – for satellite TV, phones, and you may be adding new ones such as electricity cables (for water pumps, sound systems, computers, telephones, lights), or water pipes for irrigation systems.

All of these will have to be hidden above ground somehow. You begin to see why decking is such a great choice – all of those wires can go under the deck.

Storage

It's pretty much guaranteed that you will need storage – and that it will be easier to store stuff outside than to bring it in.

So if at all possible make provision for some sort of cupboard outside for furniture, for any gardening and cleaning bits and bobs. Just a seat with a hinged top is a great way to have storage yet save on space. Or, at the other extreme, you can make a screened utility area to put everything out of sight.

Cost

Things will tend to cost more up on the roof. There will be more man-hours involved in everything that's done and because the technical requirements are stringent, there are higher costs involved in getting the project off the ground (so to speak).

It may mean that the project has to be done over time in sections. It's worth talking to the architect or builder about the most sensible way to do this.

Barriers

Planning and building regulators will be very interested in the barriers around the garden, but even beyond this it's worth thinking carefully about the barriers and their maintenance, especially if children are going to use the roof.

Not only should the barrier be solid but there should be no way that the kids can climb up or over it. Containers near the barrier, toys, a fire escape, seats – all of these could be used by a climbing child who's inquisitive to see what's over the wall. I know I'm paranoid about this, but also keep checking on the condition of the barriers – a loose screw or a bit of rust can make a barrier unsafe.

Load-bearing areas

Always get a structural engineer to give precise details about what can be put where.

As a very rough guide, around the edge and above internal supporting walls will probably be where it's safer to put heavy loads like planters, seating areas and water features. These areas which can take a heavier load may well define the design and dictate the layout.

TAKE ADVICE … It really is worth getting a proper survey done not just to avoid disaster, but also to point up some solutions to problems as well.

Contradictions of roof gardens

Light v secure

All advice is to go lighter – lighter containers, lighter furniture, lighter materials – but lighter is more likely to blow over and away. So go for light but make sure it's securely fastened down (without damaging the waterproofing of the roof).

Privacy v view

You want privacy and screening but you also want to make the most of the great views. If you want 360-degree views, it's going to be a windy and exposed place and perhaps not one you'd want to spend hours in. As ever, probably the best solution is to compromise. Find where the prevailing winds are coming from, screen an area from these, and if you're lucky, the view out will be the other way.

Gathering information

O nce you've put down information about the technical issues specific to gardening on high, the process of designing a terrace or roof garden is very much like designing any other garden.

The next step is to get together more general information about what's there and some input about what you want from the garden.

What is there?

A lot of information about the site will have come out in the purely practical section in Chapter 1, but now we are looking at your space in aesthetic and functional terms rather than for technical reasons. I've put below a list of common features that you may find and next to them the possible implications these would have on the design. There may be other things you notice, specific to your garden, but a lot of the issues will be common to all gardens on high.

Feature	Impact on design
Will the garden be viewed from inside the house? And if so from where?	If there's a large window or door overlooking the garden it's worth thinking carefully about this view. It will be seen all day every day, winter and summer, so it needs to look good – in fact this view will probably be the most continually seen part of the garden.
When you are in the garden is there any particular view out to the wider world that needs to be enhanced or any bad view that needs to be screened?	Screening, using plants or trellis, can hide bad views. Also these same materials can both lead the eye to, and frame, good views.
Is the garden overlooked?	If the garden is overlooked, an overhead structure or a taller tree might help to screen at least part of it. Perhaps the part that you intend to sit in and use the most.

| **Does the site have an uneven surface or level changes?** | Level changes add interest to the garden but can be a pain if they are right where you want a table and chairs. Try to even out at least this area by taking the higher level across, perhaps using decking. Decking will also transform uneven surfaces into a flat plane. |

| **Is the garden very sunny and open?** | You will probably want some shade in the garden, even if it's just a sun sail to take the worst of the midday heat off, but you may want to bring in more substantial shade with a built structure which will also keep out the wind. |

Sun sails are easy to put up if the sun becomes too hot and look great in an urban environment. This garden is by Urban Roof Gardens.

| **Or are there areas of deep shade?** | If there are shady areas then try to make a feature of them with leafy, shade-loving plants and a seat hidden amongst the foliage. At night this can all be lit – the lights hidden in the greenery. |

| **Are there ugly things on the roof like satellite dishes, storage units?** | Hide these with screens, trellis or planting – this may help determine the layout of your space. |

This trellis from the Garden Trellis Company is perfect for screening and keeping out the wind.

Drawing up a plan

Gathering information about the site might also include measuring it up and doing a plan. When you are redesigning an area it does help to do a plan on paper. You can make lots of copies and pretty much endlessly change these without setting anything in concrete. Also, if it's to scale, the drawing will give you the exact proportions of all the items and the overall space so you can place things accurately.

As well as the overall dimensions and measurements within the garden, put on the plan everything that is there now and will stay, for example,

- Outline of the garden
- Outbuildings that will stay, like shed

- Access points to the garden
- Drains
- Level changes
- Outside taps
- Power sources.

You don't need to bother measuring things you know will be going.

Also mark on the plan good and bad things – a good view, an eyesore, a sheltered spot, a sunny spot etc.

Of course if you can't do a plan, or don't want to do one, it's possible to mark things out on the ground with tape – it will be more immediate and easier to imagine.

What do you want?

The other bit of information gathering to do before the design begins is to note down what you want from the space.

1. Do you want to be secluded and alone, or do you want the space to accommodate parties?

The garden can do both but you may want to prioritise one over the other. For example, if you want …

A garden for entertaining – a public space

You might have

- A central, large outside eating area
- Lots of places to sit and open areas
- A barbecue
- Heaters (braziers or fire pits are more environmentally sound than gas heaters)
- Sound systems
- A hot tub or sauna
- Lights.

A garden for seclusion – a private space

- Single seats
- A hideaway of timber or trellis, with a great view out but hidden from the rest of the world
- Planting and screens to create intimate areas
- Power and phone points to plug computer into and set up ipod
- A hot tub or sauna – to make the most of the privacy and the view.

2. Sitting areas – how big and where should they be?

- Sitting areas might be a single seat for private contemplation or a table for 12.
- If you want to have a table and chairs make sure the space is big enough – you need room for the table, room for the chairs, room for people to sit on the chairs and then room for people to get around the back.

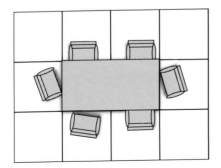

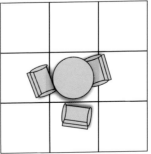

1 square = 1metre²

2

- As well as the size of the area needed, whether it's in sun or shade is a big decision. It's logical to put the sitting area in the sun – you can always bring in shade as you need it.
- But think about where the shadows are going to be cast from a sunshade or sail. A parasol set in the centre of the table will be great at midday in midsummer; the rest of the time the shade is likely to overshadow the table too much and be no good for those sitting round it.
- Perhaps more important is to have the seating area out of any wind.

- But if there's a place for seats that has a particularly good view, I think this trumps everything else. You can put a shade up and a shelter for wind – you can't recreate the view.

Is it weird?

If you do put the sitting area right next to the house, and there's a sitting area just inside, there may be a problem. Some people think it looks strange to have one set of table and chairs inside and one outside – right next to each other on each side of the glass. I never thought it seemed weird at all until someone pointed it out to me – now it does.

3. Practical things like washing lines, electricity, water needed and to where on the roof?

- **Electricity**
  Even if you don't want lights or any other electrical equipment on the roof right now, put in ducting – empty pipes – around the garden through which wires can be threaded later without having to disturb any paving or decking.

- **Washing line**
  You may need a washing line – there are some pretty smart ones available now but an old-fashioned line strung across a roof has a lot going for it. Not too far away and in the sun is usually the best place for a washing line.

- **Compost**
  It is usually a good idea to have somewhere to put any garden rubbish, although if there are only a couple of plants it's probably not worth it. It needs to be out of sight and away from sitting areas.

- **Storage**
  The chances are you will need storage – for cushions and cleaning equipment and if there are children then there will probably be toys to hide away.

- **Water**
  If you have any number of plants at all, an outside tap will be really helpful when it comes to watering them, and from that tap you can also run an automatic irrigation system.

4. Easy movement between inside and out or a surprise?

If you are creating a new terrace or roof garden and have control over the access and movement between inside and out, it's worth trying to make this access as easy as possible and making the views from inside as wide and uninterrupted as possible. Something like floor to ceiling glass and doors that open right back is ideal. Every time you want to carry your food outside, you will thank yourself for the decision. Every time you look out to the garden and get the sense of space from the skyline and the sky above, you will thank yourself.

But if that's not possible and access is up a ladder or staircase, work on the element of surprise – the 'wow' factor as you enter the garden.

Can you see the garden from the inside?

If you do have great views across the garden from inside the house, it will need to look good all year round. Evergreen plants, strong structure and good lighting will help. If you can't see out to the garden from the house, chances are you won't go out there that often in winter, so concentrate on getting it looking good from spring through to autumn.

Creating spaces

All the information is in about the site and how you want to use it – it's now time to draw it all together.

You can do this in two stages:

1. Firstly, think about your inspiration, getting the look and tone of the garden.
2. Secondly, about actually designing the garden – making the space.

Inspiration

It's very useful to look at pictures of other roof gardens and terraces to see which ones appeal to you. You don't have to copy them exactly but look at the elements which attract you; it may be shady green spaces, clean uncluttered lines, a sense of mystery. These are things to bring to the plan of your garden. The second half of this book is full of inspiration. You can also use a theme …

Design themes

Is a theme a good thing? Will it be a pastiche? Doing the 'full Disney' is not going to work for everyone … although I have done a garden with that very requirement as part of the brief and, though I say so myself, I think it worked very well. On safer ground, you might want a touch of the Mediterranean, a colour theme, or take inspiration from modern gardens. These types of themes can be great to give direction to a garden and an overall spirit to it. A theme helps you decide how to design it and how to decorate it. The best way to avoid clichés is to tread lightly with the theme – to take inspiration and apply touches rather than slavishly recreate. The other tip is to only put things into the garden where they are necessary to the function of the design. Adding lots of sculpture willy-nilly will look overdone, whereas one piece used as a focal point will give direction to the garden.

This piece by David Harber has the weight to carry an area without overpowering it. It's made of smooth pebbles formed into a perfect circle – at night it's lit from inside so shafts of light sparkle out from it.

When you are looking for inspiration think about the question below which will help enormously in giving direction to the garden:

Fit with interior or be a surprise?

Sympathetic and in keeping with the building? Or a surprise, a 'wow'? There aren't any rules about this but generally speaking I think it's best to maintain the lines of the building. So if it's a really modern building have strong lines in a similar material. Where you can make the surprise is in the planting. Rather than have modern, minimalist planting, put in fluffy meadow plants with loads of flowers. Kept in the stark beds they will look great. Similarly, if you have a more traditional building, elements of the modern can be brought into the terrace or rooftop with a stainless-steel sculpture or a very modern, minimalist water feature, but that's just an opinion and one of the great things about gardens is that you can express yourself, create your own world and make your 'wow'.

Linking inside and out

If you do want to visually link the inside and the out there are a few more ways to help:

1. Materials

If you have sharp rendered walls in light colours inside, use the same crisp colours outside. The space will seem to continue onwards and outwards and look much bigger. Similarly if there are floorboards inside the house, use decking boards outside. If there are floor tiles inside, use a similar tile outside. If the material has a pattern to it, use the same pattern and the same direction inside and out.

Same materials inside and out?

Be careful about using exactly the same materials. Often these will weather more quickly outside and within a year look completely different from those indoors.

2. Colour and pattern

Continuing the same colours and patterns outside will also help to join the two spaces together and make the one area look bigger. For example:

- Paint the walls outside the same colour as the walls inside.
- Use the same fabric patterns on sunshades outside that you have on light shades inside.
- Furniture colours can be repeated in both areas.

3. Overheads to link inside and out

I have to say I don't think these are a good idea when attached to the house. In this country we are so short of light that overhead structures right next to the building will cut out too much of the daylight coming through the windows, but if you can live with that, try going for wires or thin wood with a deciduous climber over to give extra shade in summer but blocking less light in winter. The effect of the overhead will be to continue the ceiling line of the room inside outward and so make it look bigger.

4. Decorative elements continued between inside and out

- For a really exciting effect take a flow of water from the inside out. A channel like this, lit from below and leading out into the night, is a breathtaking feature.
- Using the same types and patterns of lighting can also help to smudge the transition between inside and out, helping to make the space seem a single room, open to the sky.
- The same containers placed at regular intervals and lit from below can be placed in a line going from inside to out.

Geometrical versus informal design

If straight lines, strong geometrical shapes and symmetry inspire you, you will get a very different garden from one inspired by informal shapes, loose lines and asymmetry.

How to get a geometrical design

1. Strong, simple lines

- This often works best in the urban setting where there are strong lines all around the garden.
- It tends to make a formal garden with very strong structural elements.
- Use evergreens to enhance the structure of the hard landscaping and design. Clipped yew and box, bamboo. These will give year-round structure to the garden and will look after themselves to a large degree.

2. Symmetry

One way to create symmetry is to find a central axis and create the rooms on either side of this.

3. Repetition

Use repeating patterns to give another geometrical element to the design. A rhythmic pattern of planters or overheads will give a great structural, architectural element to the design.

4. Minimalist

Taking the clutter out of the garden and having a really strong geometry to the layout will lead you to minimalism.

Minimalist gardens

These work beautifully on roof gardens and terraces. They have an architecture, a simplicity and clarity to them that goes with urban environments, but at the same time that architecture is ordered and very calm. It's the place you can contemplate a single leaf or the way the light falls across a wall.

They are also nicely low maintenance – a brush over and they are as good as new.

How to make a minimalist garden?

- Minimalist gardens rely on beautiful, balanced design with a strong architecture.
- If the garden is too open at the sides it may just look empty, so you may need to put in walls to enclose the spaces.
- The proportions of these spaces have to be spot on and it's important to think carefully about how those spaces are created. The clean lines of walls or a single type of plant like bamboo often work well.
- Add nothing to this layout unless you *really* have to and think very carefully before you do.

Minimalist gardens work incredibly well on roofs and terraces

1. You will only need a few plants so it works with the limited soil. You may only need one beautifully shaped tree or a line of bamboo to introduce greenery into the space.

2. Minimalism takes its strength from its boundaries. It needs the enclosure for the proportions to work and clean clear walls and floors are perfect for an enclosed roof or terrace.

3. Those pure clean planes of walls and floors will also give great shadows – both from the strong sunlight on the roof and from artificial light after dark.

4. Seating is an issue for minimalism and it's best to have in-built seating that reinforces the architecture. This seating is also great for roof gardens because it won't blow away and can give you storage under the lids.

Informal

It is possible to have an informal garden on a roof, but from a design point of view it doesn't grow out of the situation as well as, say, a minimalist garden.

If you do want something less formal I would try to keep the shapes strong and clear but soften them with what you put around and in the shapes. Use, for example …

- Massed plantings
- Rustic materials
- Hidden areas
- Colourful cushions
- Coloured lights or tealights.

PUTTING IT TOGETHER

Wherever you draw your inspiration from, when you apply it to your garden you are creating spaces – the art of garden design is the art of making spaces.

Dividing up the area

A roof garden or terrace is pretty much the archetypal 'outside room'. It will tend to be smaller than the ordinary garden; it will have a solid floor (hopefully) and may well have walls on two or more sides – basically, a room. How would you design a space like this inside the house? Well it wouldn't look good just to scatter sofas and tables about hopefully. Inside you would naturally create a sitting area and maybe a dining area and once those areas had been defined you would decorate and add lighting. Well outside the same rules apply.

This is probably the first, last and only rule of garden design that you really need to know.

Divide the space, create zones, don't just scatter elements around, use really strong shapes to create rooms. Obviously these rooms have to be made within the boundaries but they don't have to follow them. It's more important to make a good shaped room than to relate the living areas to the external boundaries.

All of those books called 'garden rooms' or 'the outside room' are going on about something completely fundamental to making gardens. If you make spaces within the garden's boundaries and make these spaces into lovely rooms, perhaps fill the space that's left around the edges with planting, you will pretty certainly get a good strong design.

Rooms – why?

Apart from making beautiful spaces to be in, designing this way has all sorts of benefits for the layout of the garden.

1. Make rooms for different purposes and you make sense of the space

If your roof garden or terrace is large enough it would be great to create rooms with different purposes, a sitting room, a dining room, a study, a Jacuzzi room. Even if they aren't completely screened off, low implied divisions will help to make sense of the space.

2. Create mystery and surprise

A space that can all be seen at once is much less interesting than one you can discover. In a smaller space like a terrace the possibilities for surprise are fewer but even a simple trellis reaching halfway across can give an element of mystery and a reason to explore.

3. Shelter This is where the design gets really clever. Those rooms will also come with vertical divisions that not only define the space, they also shelter that space from the wind. Put a gap in the wall, like a window if there's a good view.

4. Hide things Those divisions can be used to hide things like satellite dishes, storage areas or a bad view.

5. Focal points The rooms can hold focal points which will help to draw the eye and form view stoppers. Beyond an entrance to a 'room' is a perfect place to put a focal point.

6. Create directional movement If you encourage people to explore the garden and take people on a journey through it, even if it's just from one divide to the next, the garden will seem larger and more interesting than one that is all on view at once.

7. Conceal the overall shape of the garden

This is especially important if that overall shape is unpleasant. A long terrace which, when you're in it, feels like sitting in a corridor, will feel much better if it's divided up to make smaller rooms with better proportions.

Walls & floors

Once you've decided where to place divides or create new rooms, the next question is how to do this? Both the vertical and the horizontal elements of the garden will help to create the spaces and make them real.

Verticals

Boundaries

On a roof or terrace there are the boundaries and the internal screens. They will have features in common but the external boundary screens obviously have an important safety element to them which may dictate how they are made and what they look like.

Specific to external boundaries

1. Are they already in place and passed as safe?
2. Local regulations will apply, do check.
3. If in doubt consult a professional.
4. On the boundaries, safety is the main concern. They need to be high enough and strong enough to prevent possible accidents.

5. They should also give shelter and screening from winds.
6. They should allow and control water runoff.
7. If the boundary fencing is purely functional and not very pretty, it is possible to create a screen on the inside of it which is more decorative (with the usual caveats about weight and water runoff).

Planning regs ...
The height of any permanent boundary and permanent structure will be dictated by local building regulations.

Screens – 9 practical points

1. Divides don't have to be above eye level to be effective – implied divisions can be quite low and will allow you to see through to different areas but still give the impression of different spaces.

2. But obviously for privacy you will need higher screens.

3. Plants like bamboo, trees, tall shrubs or hedges, low and high, can divide up spaces.

4. If you're planting a hedge, the larger the plants you put in the more quickly you will get an instant effect, but make sure they are secure. A tall new hedge may need help to keep it from toppling in wind.

5. If you have a solid fence or wall the winds will rise up and over … and down again – they create turbulence. Something less solid will slow the wind down and make a more effective break.

6. So as well as being more suited to the weight restrictions of a roof or terrace, fences and trellis will provide a permeable barrier that will make a better windbreak.

7. If you do use solid panels, leave gaps between.

8. The verticals need to be firmly secured – but you must be careful not to puncture the waterproofing on the roof.

9. Think about access – long pieces of wood might not fit in the lift or go around the stairwell.

This screen from the Garden Trellis Company allows the wind to filter through, slowing rather than stopping it.

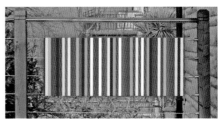

You can add your own style to any barrier – this canvas is from Cheeky Mojito.

Materials & style

If you have a theme to your garden – and you probably will have one even if it's something as subtle as 'modern' – this will influence the style of the verticals.

Type	Style
Close board fencing painted in chalky colours	Scandinavian or seaside
Expanded mesh, perforated metal sheets in copper, steel	Ultra modern. Stainless steel will stay shiny; galvanised will take a grey patina; copper will tarnish green
Painted marine ply or battens, repeated pattern of modern containers with plants	Slick and modern
Trellis, yew hedges, pleached trees, repeated pattern of traditional terracotta pots with plants	Traditional formality, Arts and Crafts
Espaliered fruit trees, tall shrubs	Country, informal
Bamboo and woven willow	Japanese – these will have to be replaced every few years
Canvas screens, pulled taut like sails	Nautical and colourful
Toughened glass screen framed with stainless steel	To maximise the views and give a modern look
Translucent sheets of polycarbonate framed in steel	Quirky and modern, these create interesting shadows and colours

- These verticals don't just divide up the garden. Like walls in a house they can hold lights and decorations – murals, mosaics and water features.

- It's also great to experiment with creating openings in the screen to niches or to views of the rest of the garden or beyond the garden's boundaries.

Vertical structures

4

These may be for decoration, for storage, for shelter from the wind or most likely for shade on the roof. They will add to the vertical boundaries of the roof and should be built into the design.

Shade awnings Sun sails are architectural and fit with the ambience of many roof gardens.

Bower from wood This is more suited to a traditional, informal garden.

Tents are very trendy Easy to put up and maintain, and perfect for entertaining and relaxing.

Arches If they are wooden they look traditional, made of metal they look more modern. Either wood or metal they give a vertical element up which to grow plants.

Pergolas Covered walkways are great to give definition to areas and provide a sheltered, shady, dry place to sit and walk.

Arbour/summer house/gazebo Whatever you call it it's great to have something enclosed, heated and with lights – but with lots of glass so you can use it all year round and be right out there with the sky and the elements.

Framing views …

Most people who have a good view want it to be completely uninterrupted and it's difficult to argue with that. If you have the most glorious panorama of a city it's difficult to see how it can be improved, but most views can be. Coming across a view gives it more impact; having a frame around it will give it focus and meaning. It's worth thinking about taking control of the view.

Floors

This is one of the most important elements in the design and often one of the most neglected. On a roof you have to consider first and foremost the practical aspects of the floor, like the weight of the materials and whether you can get them up to the roof. Then consider its visual impact – the wrong floor can give out all the wrong signals.

Think back to the theme or the ethos of the garden that you want to create – however gently you intend to impose this. Modern and light, Japanese, traditional? Also look at the floor inside the building – if it's near to the floor outside it might be good to take a cue from that and continue the same look of material and patterns.

Design

Patterns

The way you lay or arrange the flooring materials has a bearing on apparent space.

- Strong lines tend to draw your eye in their direction.
- If you want to make the space seem wider and slow the eye down, lay the boards or slabs across the area.
- Small elements – bricks or small tiles – will feel lighter and buzzy.
- Fewer different things, especially in a small area, will increase the feeling of space. Filling it up with various patterns, colours and materials will make it feel cluttered and closing in.

Materials

Heavy materials such as stone or tiles may be out of the question if there are restrictions on weight, if the existing surface is very uneven or if getting materials up to the roof is a problem. Decking is, generally speaking, an ideal surface for a roof garden.

Wet floors will get slippery ...

Any solid floor, if it is in the shade and not drying out well, will become slippery in wet weather.

Decking

Benefits

- It's a floating structure so it can
  - Hide imperfections
  - Conceal level changes
  - Create level changes for interest
  - Hide cables and wires underneath
- It's light and its weight can be transferred to the roof at the best points
- It's a relatively inexpensive material
- It's relatively easy to lift if there's a problem with the roof underneath
- It's easy to cut to size and to cut out shapes around chimneys
- Hardwoods, like ipe, will take on a silvery grey tint after a while outside and will look more natural
- There are lots of opportunities for sunken lighting and using LED lights.

Disadvantages

- Hardwoods may not be environmentally sound –make sure it comes from a renewable resource
- Decking boards can be long and may not go in a lift or round the bend of stairs
- If you paint or seal the wood it will need re-doing every year or so
- It can be slippery if water stays on the surface for a long time.

Don't block water runoff ...

Make sure that drainage is not blocked by any of the boards of the decking.

Stone

Stone can give a more traditional look to a garden and has a wider variety of finishes.

The main disadvantages of stone are:

- More expensive
- Heavier
- Can be slippery.

Leave it to breathe …

The whole surface is likely to contract and expand with temperature changes so it needs a little give. If the paving is set securely onto the roof, things will crack. Use flexible filler or expansion joints at regular intervals.

Limestone	The main issue with limestone is that it stains; French limestone is less porous so will keep its light colour better.
Marble	Expensive but very durable and comes in a huge range of colours.
Granite	It can be used in setts or stones or a mixture of the two.
Slate	Riven (split along natural lines) ,it looks traditional. Sawn, it looks very modern.
Gravel	The cheapest option – cheap to buy, cheap to lay.
Resin bound gravel	More expensive than loose gravel but a sharper look and the gravel won't go everywhere.
Pebbles, stones	Combine these with gravel for an interesting textured surface.
Tiles	The range of tiles available is enormous and they are well suited to roof gardens – bridging the gap between inside and out.
Rubber tiles	For a kooky modern garden.
Fake grass	Don't dismiss this – fake grass is getting very realistic and it could be a great solution for a roof or terrace.
Industrial flooring	There's an exciting world of flooring out there that's been designed for workplaces and factories. It can give a wonderful modern feel to the roof – metal mesh, extruded and punched metal, fibreglass. One word of caution – metal flooring will get hot in the sun.

Containers

Roof gardens and terraces vary enormously in size, aspect, style – the one thing they all have in common is they are above ground level so they have no natural soil. Any plants will have to grow in soil or some other medium that's been brought up to the site.

There are three ways to do this:

1. Containers – stand alone objects, usually moveable, filled with compost.

2. Raised beds – built-in beds which are usually large enough to replicate the same growing conditions as a flower bed at ground level.

3. A growing medium – these are high tech 'substrates' which are specially designed to be spread across roofs. Most often they are millimetres thick to hold low-growing plants but they can be deeper to allow a wider range of plants to grow. The use of plants over so much of the roof is usually called a green roof or a living roof (see Chapter 10).

It always amazes me that people who don't like gardening, who truly desire a low-maintenance garden, will still want containers in the garden. Why do people like containers? Well they seem easy, you know where you are with them and you can look after them in seconds, but most importantly of all they offer several chances to shop. You can buy the containers, buy the plants and when they die, buy the plants again.

Advantages of growing in containers

- Very little weeding – the soil is clean and there's not much bare soil surface to let weeds grow.
- Easy to feel in control – they tend to be small so it's easy to keep on top of them.
- You can create lovely displays.
- It's possible to move the containers around – you can create different seasonal effects with them.
- To liven up areas away from the ground – because they are raised, the plants will be taller than if they were just in the ground.
- To hide nasty areas – they are great for use as a screen.

Disadvantages

- They are not maintenance free.
- They need watering and feeding.
- If they aren't heavy they may fall over.
- If they are heavy they may cause structural problems if positioned in the wrong place.

5

Design with containers

Uses for containers

If you place containers with a purpose they are more likely to look right – to look like they belong in the garden and haven't just been plonked there. Here are some possibilities …

1. To punctuate a wall – a long wall can look quite boring and possibly oppressive. Put a repeated row of tall containers along it, possibly lit from below at night, and the look is transformed.

2. To announce an entrance – at either side of any entrance containers will look like they belong.

3. To mark out an area – they can help to form rooms and delineate areas within the garden.

4. To provide screening – the extra height the container gives to any plant will help it to give a higher screen.

5. To provide a focal point – one container to focus and draw the eye can help to make sense of a room. It needs to be big enough to be noticed though and in proportion to the space.

Design tips

- If in doubt stick to one type of plant per container – it will probably look more stylish and is easier to look after.
- Larger pots give more impact and need less watering.
- Colour in containers – think how the colour of the container will react with the leaves and flowers of the plant above.
- Think about the scale and proportion – of the container in its space and of the plant in the container.
- Repeated pots and repeated plants will give an architectural look.
- Plants with strong shapes and a sculptural appearance placed in containers can reinforce that architectural effect.
- If an area is unbalanced – say with a seating area to one side – you may need something on the other side of a view to visually balance it up. Containers are one way to do this.
- Creating symmetry, rhythm and order. Using several of the same containers in rows can give symmetry to a design and impose order on a space. They need to be quite big to influence the look of an area, but they can help to give a minimalist, modern feel to a garden.

Practical tips

Containers need to

- Retain moisture in the soil
- Be free-draining – so holes in the bottom of the pot are essential
- Withstand ice and high temperatures – the freeze/thaw cycle will cause many containers to crack as water gets into any gaps and freezes causing the material to 'blow'.

Standing containers on 'feet' will

- Help with drainage
- Give slugs and snails a harder time
- Stop them from causing rot on the rooftop
- Help to stop the roots coming out of the pot and into the roof.

Beware wet soil …

Wet soil is really heavy, so a large planter, full of soil after a few days of rain in the winter, can pose a risk to the integrity of the roof if it's not placed carefully.

What types of plants can you grow in containers? 5

I'd say 'anything' but there are some types of plants you have to be careful with.

Problem	Solution
Very thirsty plants with big leaves	Install an automatic watering system.
Leggy plants where there's a lot of stem before you get to the leaves and flowers	Use a larger pot than you might normally do and only fill it half full of compost, so the leggy parts of the plant are hidden inside the container and all you see are the leaves and flowers.
Very big plants like trees	Enjoy them for a few years and then replace them if they start to get too big for the pot. (You can do things like root pruning but it's easier just to start afresh.)

Types of containers

What sort of pot you go for is a personal matter and perhaps dictated by the look you are going for in the garden. It's worth thinking about the disadvantages of each …

- **Terracotta pots** Prone to crack in frost, if they can be moved to a sheltered spot over winter it would be good.
- **Wooden** Because they are continually getting wet then drying out they do tend to rot.
- **Metal** Metal can allow the plant's roots to overheat in the sun – so make sure they have a double thickness so the air can insulate the roots.
- **Custom-made** Can create and define spaces more than just a single container can, but they are expensive.
- **Raised beds** Custom-made again and one step up in size from containers. So they are heavy and expensive …

Modern slick   Minimalist   Cottagey country   Formal elegance   Mediterranean

Raised beds

Raised beds are really just very big, built-in containers and, like containers, in many ways the bigger the better. It's better from a maintenance point of view – they are less likely to keep drying out – but safety has to come first and bigger will be heavier, and these are heavy, especially when full of wet soil, so check the weights with an architect or structural engineer.

Solutions to the weight problem

1. Check the placings with an architect or structural engineer.
2. Don't use soil right down to the bottom of the container, use perlite or some other light, bulky material.
3. Make sure the drainage on the containers is as good as it can be and make sure the water from the containers is going to established runoffs.

Design with raised beds

It's obviously incredibly important where these raised beds go; they will be crucial to forming the design of the garden. Hopefully their layout will have been decided at the design stage so that they will

- Be in the right place structurally
- Provide screening
- Help to make rooms
- Give a good backdrop to the garden area.

What to make them out of?

A good bet is marine ply, with a metal edging to give them the appearance of weight. They will be quite light, durable and easy to plant up.

Irrigation

It's a funny thing but half the time in container gardening you are trying to keep the water in and the other half you're trying to make sure it drains away – but such is life. Too much, and the water will pool in the bottom of the container and rot the plant's roots. Too little water, or water that shoots away too quickly, and the plant will die.

Ways to water

1. Hand watering. This is possible and many people find it quite a relaxing occupation. However, if you are going on holiday in the summer it can cause a problem.

2. A leaky hose system works well on terraces. Turn the tap on and water is taken around the garden, where it needs to water plants the hose is permeable so the water seeps out. It is easy to install but you do need to hide the hosepipe and you can do this under decking or alongside perimeter walls. There are timer systems so the hose is turned on and off even if you're away.

3. Many containers have some sort of capillary action from reservoirs in their base. This reservoir needs to be kept full but needs filling up less often than a pot without one.

Practical tips for irrigation

1. Make sure there's good drainage in any containers – put holes in the bottom if they aren't already there. If the water can't drain away it will pool in the pot and the roots of the plant will rot.

2. To help the water get away even more efficiently, put bits of polystyrene or large pebbles in the base of the pot. Now this is the advice that's always given. Myself, I'm sceptical. I think if you've got a big container and want to save on soil or weight it's a good idea to put something lighter in the bottom, but generally speaking, I don't think this improves drainage.

3. Clay pots do allow water to evaporate through their surfaces – to keep this from happening line the sides of the pot with thick plastic (perhaps from your bag of compost) and this will help the water to stick around longer.

4. Mulches – this is a layer of material (gravel, cobbles, what have you) which goes on top of the soil. The theory is that it helps to stop the soil drying out and reduces evaporation. It may do this (again, I'm sceptical; you're just replacing a depth of compost with a depth of something else and either of these will start drying out in the sun), but it certainly will make a difference to the way the container looks. If you don't like looking at bare soil, it's a great way to cover this up.

5. Where does the water go after it has left the container? If it's across paving you are likely to end up with stains. Putting a pan under each container can help but they need to be emptied regularly so they don't overflow or become a breeding place for mosquitoes.

6. Water-holding granules soak up moisture and release it slowly as the soil around them dries out.

Planting up containers

Practical tips

1. Soil – isn't the best thing to use in containers because it
- Is very heavy
- Doesn't hold water well, dries out quickly
- Will probably be full of weed seeds
- May also have diseases in the soil
- Probably won't have enough nutrients available
- And it's of variable quality.

2. It's easiest to use a specialised compost – for hanging baskets or containers. These have been developed to hold water well, are clean and have built-in plant food.

3. Composts straight from the bag are dry, and when wet will be much heavier – adding to the loading on the roof.

4. Compost will settle in the first few months and you may need to top up the beds.

5. If you need an even lighter compost, mix in some perlite or other lightweight filler, not too much or the compost will be too poor for the plants – 20% filler is maximum.

6. Make sure the container is big enough for the plant to be happy and to grow. It must hold sufficient compost to insulate plants' roots from frost during the winter and to sustain healthy growth.

7. Keep the plant in its pot while you are sizing up the container and starting to put compost in the bottom. It will be easier to move the plant in and out of the container to see if you've got it to the right height.

8. When planting up a container make sure the plant isn't in line with the top rim of the container, make it lower by a good inch or so. It will look better (and you can play with this – if you have a leggy plant you can pot it really low so only the flowers peep over the top) but also it will give you room to pour water into the container without the whole thing overflowing.

9. Make sure the soil level is the same as it was in its original pot – higher and the roots are exposed to the air, lower and the roots are too low in the soil and not at the best position to get water.

10. You can 'tease out' the roots which apparently helps them find their way outwards, but roots depend on tiny hairs along their sides to do their work and I think touching the roots like this does more harm than good. Their purpose is to find water and nutrients – they don't need our help to realise there's some lovely stuff in the soil around them.

How to plant up a container

Emma Plunket from Plunketgardens specialises in city gardens and uses containers often on the roof gardens she designs. Here are her top tips for planting up containers.

Step 1 Check the container has a drainage hole. Fill the bottom with a lightweight material like perlite to aid drainage and keep the weight down – this is important on roof terraces and with large containers.

Step 2 Cover this with geotextile fabric (or a cloth) to prevent compost draining out of the hole or potentially blocking it.

Step 3 Next comes a little compost – make sure it's suitable for containers; many manufacturers do a special mix for containers.

Step 4 Keep the plant you want to use in its pot so that it's easy to try it for size and also to swivel round. Plants have a back and a front – make sure the best side is showing forward.

Step 5 When you have enough compost in the bottom to lift the new plant nearly to the rim, take the plant out of its pot, pop it in and fill around it with more compost.

Step 6 Make sure the whole thing is really firmed down and then water it.

Step 7 For a climber you can start if off in the right direction by tying in the long ends to wires on the wall.

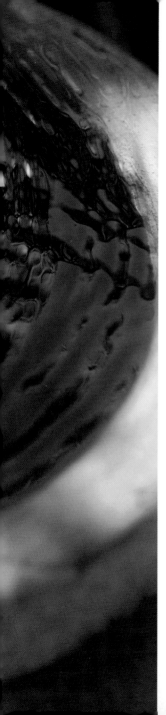

Water features

Do you need water in your garden? Well it can add to the work, the weight and the cost, but on the other hand it can also add enormously to the magic. There are so many possibilities for water – still or moving, wall mounted or a pond, modern or old fashioned – it's a really good idea to ask yourself a few questions before you start. The answers to these will help you get a feature that does what you want and looks great.

What sort of water?

Some questions …

Q: Do you want still or moving?

- Still water reflects the sky and gives a feeling of calm and a reflecting pool can be very effective especially if it's designed to be seen from the house or from a quiet sitting area. To increase the reflections make sure the pool is as dark as possible – a dark lining and black pebbles on the bottom will help.
- Moving water can give a lovely soft sound, it will catch the light and give movement to the garden.

Q: If it moves do you want the sound of water falling or spray?

- Sprays and fountains will catch the light. It's worth working out where the main viewpoint will be and where the sun will be. Ideally you want the sun behind you and the spray to get into the sun's rays.
- Fountains, and sprays in particular, can be a problem if the wind blows the water about before it reaches the basin below. At worst it can cause flooding or puddling of water; at best the water will need topping up often. Wind sensors are available to turn off the spray when the wind reaches a certain level.

Q: If you want sound – do you want a trickle or a fall?

- A small amount of water will sound like a leaky toilet, a heavier fall will, I think, sound better.
- Many modern water features have a sheet of water which comes with a really good deep sound.

Q: Do you want fish?

- Fish ponds need to be deeper than other types of pond – at least 90cm deep – to protect the fish from freezing water, and this may cause a problem where you can't dig down and are restricted with weight.
- Altogether you're probably better off with a tank indoors.

Q: Do you want to light the water?

- If you can, light under the water. This will look much better than above-water lights which shine across the surface. These just highlight any muck there.
- Make sure the light source isn't pointing towards a main viewpoint.
- Water and electricity don't mix easily – always get a qualified electrician.

Q: Do you want to buy off the peg or have it made specially?

- Off-the-peg features which will be suitable for gardens on high will include stand-alone, above-ground, enclosed units and wall features.
- Anything that involves going down into the ground, like a below-ground reservoir or pool, will require some thought. Decking can be made or cut to fit around if you know exactly which water feature you're going to have before the deck is laid.

This water feature by David Harber is beautifully integrated into its setting. The feature works with the rill of water beneath it and it is all in perfect harmony and proportion with its surrounding garden.

- If weight and budget allow, specially made features can be pretty amazing. There are endless types, but ones which work particularly well include
  - A rill, a narrow channel of water. Lit at night these look amazing when enclosing a seating area like a moat or running from the house out across the terrace or roof.
  - Raised pools are fantastic and will give architecture to a space. You can also make the sides wide enough to form extra seating.
- A sheet of water running from a letter-box opening in a wall to a pool below is a fairly ubiquitous water feature right now – but they do look good!

There are loads of ready-made water features available and the Internet is a wonderful place to buy them. You can even get hold of all the parts you need to make a modern letter-box opening feature coming out of a wall.

Tips for designing with water features

1. Choose water to suit the style of the garden. If your style is modern or traditional or quirky there will be a water feature to suit.

2. Like sculpture, water needs to be part of the design and not added on as an after-thought, so think of a good place for it while laying out the garden.

3. The water feature also needs to be in proportion to the space that it's in. If it's an open-plan garden and open to the sky, the danger is that the water feature will be lost in this huge space. Don't try to compete with the sky but either make the feature very bold so at least you notice it, or if it is smaller, put it in a more enclosed area with more confined proportions.

4. Often a simple way to make a water feature look part of the design and bring the proportions of the surrounds down to the right scale is to bed it into the garden by using plants all around it.

5. Water is very heavy and where it goes may be dictated by the weight limitations on the roof.

6. If you do have a choice about where it goes, think about whether to have a water feature near the entrance or further away. The sound of water in the distance can draw people into the garden and pique their interest, but placing it near the house or sitting area will give a point of interest and mean you can enjoy the water while sitting or from the house.

TIPS

- Make sure the electrics are done properly and the water feature is watertight.

- Chemicals can help keep the water clear as long as there's no chance of killing any plants or animals.

Sculpture

Statues and ornaments will influence the mood of the garden; more than anything else they signal its personality – but in placing them they need to appear linked to the layout and not imposed upon it. It's best to design in places to put statuary – a focal point or a view stopper, or just a corner that needs some point of interest. By marking places for objects at that early stage of the design they will look integral to the garden and not dropped on to it.

There are two different ways to place sculpture. The first is to put it in a very prominent position, the second to nestle it into the garden.

Centre stage

One large sculpture can be used to create a specific effect – to make a full stop at the end of a vista, a central feature in a formal space, provide counterpoint in an asymmetric layout.

If you want to do this …

1. The scale needs to be spot on. It needs to be quite impressive to hold its own against the sky, unless it's in an intimate area with smaller proportions; but on the other hand a piece can be too big and it may look overblown and silly.
2. If it's very prominent it needs to look good from all angles and at all times of the year.
3. Try using a cardboard cut-out to get a feel of how the piece will look in the position you are thinking of.

4. It might be worth lighting the piece so you make the most of it at night.

I have to say that placing a sculpture or ornament as a central feature takes a lot of nerve and skill. I was talking to a curator of a sculpture park the other day and even they have to reposition pieces three or four times before getting it right. In a roof garden or terrace you probably don't have the luxury of repositioning it.

Half hidden

If the sculpture isn't central you have a lot more leeway with the look, the size and the position.

1. If a sculpture is nestled in the planting its proportions are not so important.
2. If pieces are half hidden you can have more of them without making the place look littered. The rule is to only have one sculpture visible at one time as you move through the garden (although rules, as they say, are there to be broken).

TIPS

- If you're going for a big piece – worry about the weight, that it's secured, safe, and you can get it onto the terrace or roof in the first place.

- Mix art and water to get reflections, this can be especially effective if the sculpture is lit at night.

What works as sculpture

- Commission a piece – a less expensive way is to commission from a recent art graduate.
- *Objets trouvés* often make wonderful and inexpensive decorations.
- Use topiary to make a living sculpture.
- The Internet is a great source of sculpture.

Lighting

Lighting can give two different gardens – one by day, one by night. It is a huge resource of enjoyment and entertainment that is sorely under-used.

But it is beginning to come into its own.

Often people think this is because we are eating outside more or because evenings are warmer. Although these may have some impact, more important are changes that are happening away from gardens …

1. People don't have curtains any more, and even if they do, they don't draw them at night, so we are becoming aware of the darkness outside.
   A case of interior design leading exterior design.
2. New builds, new conservatories, and new extensions onto houses at ground level and above, tend to have huge windows; again these create a black canvas at night that needs to be filled.
3. There is also a case of supply stimulating demand. The more we see gardening as a shopping opportunity the more retailers are catering to us with a huge range of lights. The bigger and more accessible this range, the more people are tempted to buy.

The implications of these …

1. One of the major reasons to light the garden will be to get a good view from one side – from inside the house. In effect the garden will be a stage at night.
2. Remote controls for garden lights are available, so you can switch on the show from inside or out.
3. There are hundreds of really exciting light fittings available.

Design tips — lighting

1. Don't go overboard. Just highlight the bits you like – let the darkness work for you and hide anything you don't like.

2. Try staggering the lights as they go off into the distance. These lights can lead you bodily through the garden or lead your eye as you view the garden from inside the house; a sort of subtler version of airport landing lights.

3. Think about where the garden will be viewed from and make sure the lights look good from these points. On a roof or terrace, the main viewpoint may be from inside the house.

4. It's good not to see the light source, which will probably be blinding, so point the light away from the viewpoints.

5. For a modern look go for repeated patterns of lighting, say uplighting at regular intervals along a wall or uplighting a line of containers.

6. If you have walls, or any flat surfaces, think about creating effects by skimming lights across them or creating shadows and silhouettes on the surfaces.

7. Don't restrict fairy lights to Christmas, they look magical when wrapped around a tree trunk and scattered through a pergola or the branches of a tree.

8. If there's nothing really apparent to light, just go for a glow. Hide the lights in the foliage, it's a pretty sure-fire way of getting a good ambient lighting scheme.

9. There are quite a few colours of lights available although so far the colours themselves aren't particularly wonderful or subtle. If you do want colours I would stick to two different colours at a time. Red and blue work well, especially in a modern garden.

TIP

Mood lighting for gardens is available – where you change the colours to suit your mood.

10. Take heart, lighting will improve things. Pretty much whatever you do and wherever you put the lights – it's going to look better than darkness.

TIP

If you are stuck get a lighting designer in to help with ideas.

Practical tips

- Even if you don't put in lights when you are overhauling the roof or terrace, try to make sure at least ducting for cables is installed, so that later you can pull through lighting cables.
- Lights recessed into step risers or at the side of steps will be an important safety feature.

- Lighting can improve the security of the garden.
- Don't puncture the waterproof membrane on the roof with a spike light. Special attachments are needed for lights on roofs.
- Most outdoor lights are on a low voltage system. So you need a transformer to take mains voltage down to 12 or 24 volts. This allows for flexible cables to be taken around the garden.
- LED lights are great for gardens – they don't get hot so are safer for children, and plants won't get scorched.

Types of light

There are two types of lighting, built-in lighting systems, or stand-alone ones – just lanterns, fairy lights, candles and solar lights.

Solar lighting

These absorb the sun's energy through a panel on the top to charge a battery. There's a trade-off between brightness and battery life. Generally speaking, the longer the battery life the dimmer the light.

Mains lighting

If you're going for an electric, built-in system there are some things it may be helpful to know.

Types of lighting effect

Pretties – just for looks

Amenity – so you can do things in the garden

Safety – so people don't fall down the stairs

Security – so the burglars can see what they are doing.

Types of beam

Narrow spot – 6 to 12 degrees

Spot – beam up to 30 degrees

Flood – beam between 30 and 45 degrees

Wide flood – beam of about 60 degrees

Very wide flood – beam up to 80 degrees

Types of fitting

8

- **Uplighter** Shines up to indicate a route, emphasise a feature, project shadows. This usually works best if the light is caught on something, so you're not just lighting the air. These can be mounted on a spike but be careful not to puncture the waterproof membrane on a roof with the spike.
- **Recessed uplighter** Designed to be buried in the ground or set into hard landscaping. Some of them don't have a directional fitting, so they only shine upwards, rather than slightly to the side so you can light a wall or a plant.
- **Wall washer** Designed to go low down on a wall, it's a recessed uplighter fitted with a cowl or lens to spread the beam over a wide but controlled area of the wall.
- **Downlighter** These shine downward. So, mounted at the top of a wall they will bring out its texture. Repeated at regular intervals along a wall they give a great geometry of light.
- **Path lighter** These are specifically to illuminate paths, steps, terraces or driveways.
- **Recessed path lighter** Fitted at ground level like landing lights to mark the path.

Plants

You can try any plant on a roof garden, but it makes sense to think about the basic conditions you have. It's probably sunny, probably quite dry and may, if you don't have good windbreaks in position, be quite windy.

Top plants for roof gardens

Tall

Castor oil plant A handsome, evergreen shrub

Laurustinus Perfect evergreen for a shady spot

Hornbeam A hedging plant which will tolerate a little dryness in the soil

Smoke bush Great purple leaves and airy flowers in late summer

Bamboo Tall, takes up little ground room, evergreen, elegant.

Medium

Silver bush Fabulous silver foliage with white flowers in summer

Cabbage palm These palms come in shades of purples, oranges and yellows

Senecio Grey leaves and yellow flowers

Box Low-growing and easy to cut into shapes or form into a low hedge

Geraniums These will die as soon as there's a frost but through the summer they will provide tons of colour.

Small

Hellebore Pretty, saucer-shaped flowers in the depths of winter

Plantain lily With big showy leaves, this dies away in winter and will come back next spring

Black lily turf Slow-growing, black, grass-like plant

Ice plant You can leave the dried flower heads through the winter

Cyclamen Low-growing autumn flowering bulb.

Plants for a Mediterranean garden

A Mediterranean-type garden is perfectly suited to the conditions generally found on roofs. The plants tend to like it sunny and dry. The two things these plants don't like which you might have in your garden are wet and cold winter soil. The answer to that is to make sure the containers or beds drain really well. The other problem may be wind; if there are strong winds blowing about you'll need to think about putting up windbreaks to protect these plants.

One of the great things about this list is that they're all evergreen, so your garden will look great all year round.

Spanish dagger A tall plant with stiff, evergreen leaves

Olive tree Slow-growing tree with grey-green leaves that stay throughout the year

Lavender Grey-green leaves and purple scented flowers

Century plant A shorter, stouter version of Spanish dagger with spikes on its leaves

Vines You may not get grapes but the stems and leaves make a great show

Rosemary Evergreen taller than lavender with purple flowers early in the year

Sage A small evergreen shrub with scented leaves

Stone pine This will grow to be quite tall so it's the sort of thing which may need to be replaced when it outgrows the container

Star jasmine Evergreen climber with scented white flowers in summer

Rock rose An evergreen plant with rose-like flowers in summer.

Green roofs

The more crowded and polluted our cities become, the more demand is growing for environmentally-friendly roofs. On a large scale these can breathe life into an environment; on an individual scale they can provide habitats for insects and create a green window.

This green roof by Blackdown Horticultural Consultants uses sedums - the perfect plant for the shallow growing medium on these roofs.

More roof gardens …

Technically any roof with any greenery on it is a green roof and any greenery on roofs is going to have some benefits to the environment, but the term 'green roof' tends to refer to a roof specifically created for the plants rather than for people to enjoy.

Since 2000, over 30 million square metres of green roofs have been created in Germany alone.

To distinguish between the green roofs and others, a bit of jargon is used:

- **Intensive systems** are traditional roof gardens – a fairly standard garden which just happens to be on a roof.
- **Extensive systems** are primarily for plants, usually installed for ecological reasons, they have plants over the fullest extent of the roof. They tend to be lighter, so are suitable where the roof cannot take heavy loads, and tend to be self-maintaining.

This standard division is sometimes unhelpful because it sets one against the other, but there are crossover points. If the roof can take the weight of people and is large enough for them, there is no reason why you can't mix the two and use all the technological advances and environmental benefits of the extensive system but make it accessible and a lovely place to enjoy as well.

As with everything else to do with roofs the three considerations to bear in mind at every step are:

1. **Structural loading** – even a very light system will add to the load especially when holding water.

2. **Waterproofing** – the existing waterproofing membrane on the roof should be carefully checked and the work to install the roof done by a reputable contractor. Water runoff needs to be controlled also.

3. **Safety** – the system must be safe for anyone who goes onto the roof. Nothing must come away from the roof that's not meant to.

◀ If you have quite a steep pitch on the roof you can still green it up. This one by Blackdown Horticultural Consultants uses cross battens to prevent the plants slipping down.

▽ A meadow on a roof is a real treat in the summer months and great for wildlife, this potting shed roof is by Blackdown Horticultural Consultants.

Q&A

Isn't the soil or compost heavy on the roof?

Traditional green roofs use a lightweight growing material called a substrate. The thinnest and lightest can be just 2–5cm thick. This can hold low-growing plants like sedums. The thicker this layer of growing material, the taller the plants that can be grown.

If a green roof can be put onto a roof that won't take heavy loads, how do you look after it?

The idea of a traditional green roof is that once it's there, you don't need to go on it. The system is self-sustaining.

Can you have a roof for people to use but which is also good for the environment?

Putting any plants on a roof where previously there were none will help the environment, but a way to get the best of both worlds would be to use a semi-extensive roof. Most of the roof will use the same low input ideas of extensive roofs and the same lightweight substrates, but in places these could be slightly deeper, so a wider and more diverse range of plants can be grown. With 5–10cm of substrate you could grow things like wildflower meadows, small bulbs and alpines. Then, presuming the roof will tolerate the weight, you can put in seats and walkways and even put in taller plants and trees in containers around the places people will be, to create interest and shade.

Can you make a green roof on a slope?

If the roof slopes by more than 15–17% you will need horizontal battens going across the roof, or a wooden grid to stop the plants slipping. These will work up to a slope of 55%.

Why are there always sedums on roofs?

The very shallow substrates usually use sedums because they tolerate the conditions and they look after themselves.

They …

- Can cope with high temperatures and drought in summer
- Can cope with low temperatures in winter
- Are fine in high wind
- Don't have deep roots so they are fine in the shallow substrate
- Will spread and cover the whole roof
- Will spread back to cover any damaged area
- Take up water and release it into the atmosphere.

How exactly does it work?

Green roofs are quite simple – they are made up of four layers.

1. At the bottom, next to the existing roof, is a waterproof layer which will also keep the roots of the plants out of the structure.
2. Then there is a drainage layer to make sure water doesn't sit around and rot the plants or work its way into the roof structure. Light gravel-like materials are used for this.
3. A filter mat comes next to keep the drainage material separated from the substrate layer.
4. On top is a substrate layer or growing medium. Light things like crushed bricks and expanded clay granules are used for the plants to set root into.

This green roof by Blackdown Horticultural Consultants uses sedums – the perfect plant for the shallow growing medium on these roofs.

Advantages

This bit is important. The list of advantages of a roof garden is long and the more people that put them in, the more benefits will come from them.

The plants on roof gardens
- Will form a habitat for wildlife.
- Help battle pollution – the plants will trap dust, recycle carbon dioxide and absorb other pollutants.
- Can keep the air cooler and help mitigate the heat island effect created by cities and their buildings.
- Will soak up some rainfall that would otherwise run off hard surfaces.

- Insulate the building below – helping to reduce energy costs of keeping it cool or warm.
- Will help the roof underneath – surprisingly, a well-laid green roof doesn't hurt the roof of the building underneath, rather it increases its life by shielding it from the sun.
- Will absorb noise – they have been used on top of buildings under flight paths to help reduce the noise heard inside the building; the deeper the substrate the more marked the effect.
- Also visually help the environment – any piece of additional greenery in a city is going to help, but even a green roof on a garden shed looks amazing.

⚠ You can put a green roof on sheds or summerhouses – this one is by Blackdown Horticultural Consultants.

⚠ With a little more depth in the growing medium you can grow taller things like iris. This roof is by Blackdown Horticultural Consultants.

▲ In autumn the flowers have gone but the roof still looks great as it takes on autumn reds. This sedum roof is by Blackdown Horticultural Consultants.

Insulation

A study by the University of Central Florida found that green roofs shade and insulate the roof and evaporate moisture. Thus, they cool the roof, and reduce the demand for air conditioning in the building below. The maximum temperature of a conventional roof in their study was 130°F; the maximum temperature of the green roof was 91°F – a whopping difference, just think of the saving in air conditioning!

A similar study in Ottawa found that the green roof reduced average daily energy consumption in summer by 75%.

So if you have a roof or part of a roof that you don't necessarily want to use, or which is too small to use or perhaps can't be used because it can't take heavy loads, think about a green roof.

Inspiration

It's all very well having all this technical information at hand, it's quite another to feel moved to actually create something outside. Here are 10 different designs for roof gardens which have all tackled the limitations imposed and the possibilities of the sites in different ways.

Many of them are small spaces, often not much larger than a table and chairs, but by thinking about the design and the finish, the designers have made the most of the space and put an individual stamp on each one.

Colour blocks

The outside spaces at this property are a combination of a rooftop and terrace and although very different in their looks, together they form two distinct parts of a spectacular garden with an incredibly strong, well thought out and interesting design.

Before

When you see the terrace garden from above you see the different shapes laid out on the ground using a mixture of materials, water and planted beds. Together these form a strong, balanced pattern of lines, oblongs and squares.

But come down and you realise there are level changes in these patterns which give added interest to the interlocking shapes. These platforms have been created to accommodate changes in level in the garden which were already there. Rather than using steps to climb to different heights Charlotte Rowe, the designer, has created interlocking terraces at different levels which give so much more excitement and style to the garden and use the changes in levels rather than merely overcoming them.

The coloured wall panels use this same idea. Each one is at a different depth to give a texture to the composition that wouldn't be there if they were just flat against the wall.

The main problems of this garden are difficult to remember when faced with the elegant design, but it had its fair share. It was a dark, dingy well overlooked by neighbours and dominated by huge walls. By using predominantly white and light colours Charlotte has made the area much brighter. The walls have been used to great effect in the tall water feature, and above this, beautiful trellis screens off the whole garden.

Garden Plan

An outside dining area was part of the brief and Charlotte has created a separate space for a large, simple table and chairs. Again Charlotte has subtly created a division, this time using plants and pots, to make this room slightly separate from the rest of the space.

The coloured panels hold a stylish water feature. Just an added touch – the water falls out of only one side of the letter-box opening.

The coloured panels are in cool clean shades of blue and grey.

This raised area was in the garden before and rather than try to change the levels with all the expense that would have incurred, Charlotte has kept it raised and used it in the design. It also meant that the palm tree, which was already in the garden, could stay and thrive.

The complete transformation of this dingy terrace is amazing. Charlotte Rowe, the designer, used a background palette of very pale blue-grey and added colour with panels on the wall as well as the planting.

There are plants in the garden but they are used sparingly. Yes this does keep the maintenance down, but it also shows that the design by itself is good enough, even without the added bonus of plants.

Charlotte has used a change in level to give an implied division, to create a separate sitting area over the side.

Limestone squares on the ground are incredibly light and help to reflect what little light there is around the space.

▶ Charlotte has carefully integrated changes of level into the design both to add interest and create the forms from which the design is made.

▲ There's a lovely mix of old and modern in this garden. The clean white walls say 'modern' but the wisteria and window details say 'old'.

▲ Hydrangeas are wonderful plants for shady elegant courtyards. If the place is sheltered the sculptural, faded flowers should stay throughout winter.

▶ In the containers next to the pool are calla lilies which look good next to water and, if the weather is kind, will stay in leaf all through winter.

▼ There is something very special about having water under a step or bridge like this, it is integrated into the landscape around it and makes the water infinitely more interesting.

▲ The storage space for the boiler in the corner has been painted to blend in with the rest of the walls. Charlotte has clad the top of it in the same limestone as the floor below, again to integrate it into the garden. Finally she has used the shed as a plinth on which to stand three tall urns. Lit from below, they are dramatic in the day and at night.

▼ At night the garden lighting gives the garden a new feel. The coloured plinths are downlit, shadows are formed on the walls and the greenery becomes luminescent. The lighting design and products are by John Cullen Lighting.

▶ This garden is made for lighting. The flat planes of walls and the strong shapes and colours are great to make and catch shadows.

Tiny

Not all roof and terrace gardens have views out – this one, on top of a modern terrace, is enclosed on three sides by the apartment and on the other by a wall. So the good news is all those issues about wind and safety don't come so much into play (but you do still have to be very aware of load-bearing capabilities, it is still a roof). The bad news is you don't have the views and the sense of openness.

Before

So how to tackle the design? There are lessons from history. Treat this space as the Romans treated their courtyards – as cool central atria with a water feature in the centre to catch the eye and cool the air. That is the basis of this design.

The clients here needed an easy-to-look-after space and it really has to look good all year round – this garden is the view out from the sitting room, the kitchen and the entrance way to the flat. So the solution has been to place a low-maintenance water feature in the centre. It's been framed and held up on a stainless-steel cube to give it enough bulk to sustain the area. Around it the lines are simple and clean and the planting minimal and evergreen, enough to give greenery but not enough to make work. In-built seats add to the design and make seating that can be kept outside all year round; they also provide extra storage in the small space.

Garden Plan

The living areas wrap around three sides of the space – so it has to look good from all of these angles.

Pamela Johnson, the garden's designer, has placed the water feature out in the centre so it can be seen from all around. If it was against the wall it could only be seen clearly from one set of windows.

The strong lines of the garden exactly fit with the lines of the building around it. The water feature is exactly central to the three main windows which overlook the garden.

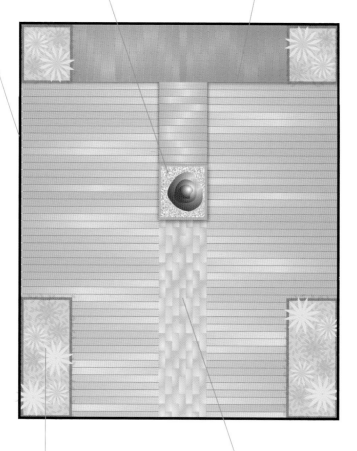

Every available wall space has been used for either seats or containers with tall plants to help soften the feel of the courtyard.

Essentially the central space has been left open but with a line across it for interest, formed on one side by the water feature and on the other by a change in the flooring.

▶ From inside the building the area looks huge. It's not, but the line of pavers stretching away from you emphasises what length there is in the scene.

▲ Often you see gardens from low down – maybe when you're sitting on the sofa – it's worth thinking about how they will look from this angle.

▶ Using a very limited range of materials draws the whole design together – red/brown hardwood and silver greys are the only colours used in the hard landscaping.

▼ Seats like this are great value. You get seating for a lot of people with no clutter. They form part of the design and help the space look bigger, and they can be used for storage which, in a tiny space, may be a huge bonus.

▲ The same wood has been used to make the raised seats as on the ground. It's a good trick to make an area seem larger; the floor doesn't abruptly stop at the back wall but carries on upwards.

▲ Next to the seat large lavenders scent the air and soften the feel of the whole area.

▼ Even in the height of summer a small space like this, surrounded by buildings, doesn't get much sun. Keeping the whole design clean and simple with a light-coloured wall along one side makes the most of what light there is.

◀ There's an interesting mix of bold architectural planting (the tall Chusan palm will stay through the winter) and below it fluffier shapes of lavender for summer scent and colour.

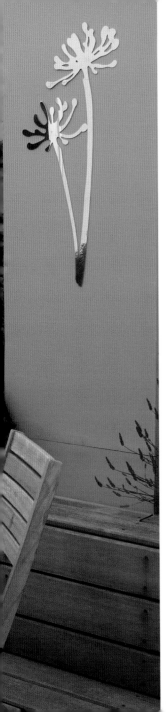

Decorating

The main walls of this space were designed and built by Site Specific, so the job of the garden designer was in effect an exterior decorating one. The roof terrace was so small that rather than redesigning the space, it was a question of making it more useful, more beautiful and more welcoming.

One of the main problems with the space was the very high wall at the back. This was originally white and looked like it was falling forwards into the space. Sara Jane Rothwell from the company Glorious Gardens redesigned the space and one of the first things she did was to paint this blue to help it recede. She also put in a built-in seat and planters right along the base of the wall to help break it up. This means the wall doesn't start right down at ground level and reach right up to the sky. Sara Jane has used the same decking on the floor as on these built-in seats; this helps to unify the area and keep down the number of different materials.

Further up the wall Sara Jane has put in climbing plants, trained along neat wires to soften the appearance of the large plane.

Lighting has also made a huge difference to the space, not only does it look wonderful after dark, it can also now be used into the night. It's these finishing touches which really make this terrace special. The underlying design is all about making a sleek and clean space; the decorations make it more welcoming. The colourful cushions from ingarden make a great contrast to the muted tones of the wall and the wall hangings give a personality to the space.

Garden Plan

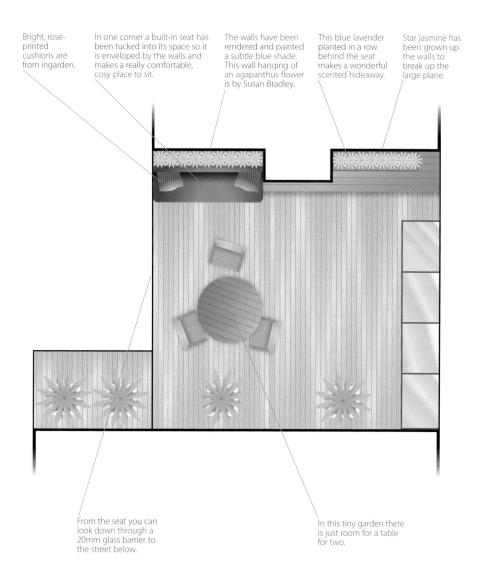

Bright, rose-printed cushions are from ingarden.

In one corner a built-in seat has been tucked into its space so it is enveloped by the walls and makes a really comfortable, cosy place to sit.

The walls have been rendered and painted a subtle blue shade. This wall hanging of an agapanthus flower is by Susan Bradley.

This blue lavender planted in a row behind the seat makes a wonderful scented hideaway.

Star jasmine has been grown up the walls to break up the large plane.

From the seat you can look down through a 20mm glass barrier to the street below.

In this tiny garden there is just room for a table for two.

▷ Rather than have railings to clutter up the scene and block the view, toughened glass provides safety without spoiling the look of the garden. On the seat are cushions from ingarden.

◀ Two beautiful acers in stylish modern pots are on either side of the entrance.

▲ Star jasmine has been trained along neat wires running across the walls.

▼ The cushions can be stored under the built-in seat.

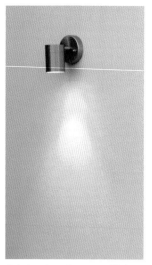

▲ A simple wall mounted light shining on a smooth rendered wall gives a great architecture of light.

◀ Another wall hanging from Susan Bradley balances up the light fitting and breaks up the expanse of the side wall.

▷ These large flat walls provide a great opportunity for spread lighting.

▽ To keep water out of the render, lead has been used to cap the top of the walls.

Entertaining

The owners of this roof terrace inherited a flat plane of decking with no structure and no greenery. They wanted a place to entertain and somewhere that had greenery throughout the year. This design by Ruth Marshall from Cool Gardens shows what can be done with containers and good design.

She has marked out different areas using huge containers. These slightly enclose the dining area and mark it as separate from the rest of the garden. The sitting area is partly covered with wires so that plants can grow up and create a shady corner. Large olive trees have been used to signal the entrance to the garden and at its corners, to give punctuation to the planting shapes. Elsewhere containers have been set into the deck so their shapes play a part in the design rather than their height, and next to the interior living space these set-down containers give planting without interrupting the view out.

The design is finished off with blue LED lights and a sound system.

The planting has been chosen to survive well in the dry and windy environment of the roof; Mediterranean plants like olives and lavenders, grey-leaved rock roses and fluffy low grasses are all able to cope with windy, dry conditions.

Garden Plan

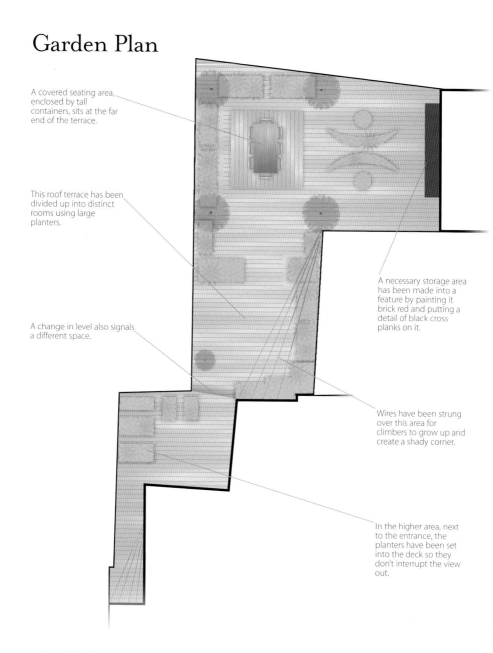

A covered seating area, enclosed by tall containers, sits at the far end of the terrace.

This roof terrace has been divided up into distinct rooms using large planters.

A change in level also signals a different space.

A necessary storage area has been made into a feature by painting it brick red and putting a detail of black cross planks on it.

Wires have been strung over this area for climbers to grow up and create a shady corner.

In the higher area, next to the entrance, the planters have been set into the deck so they don't interrupt the view out.

▶ As a subtle but important cue, Ruth has lifted the decking at the sitting area and laid it crossways to create the feeling of a different room.

▲ Tall plants like this olive have been put in the larger containers to give privacy and a feeling of enclosure to the area.

◀ Planters of powder-coated steel in geometric but asymmetrical shapes make an interesting display.

▲ In the containers that are most visible from the living areas Ruth has planted evergreen structural plants that will look good all year round.

▼ The planters were made especially for the garden from powder-coated steel and coloured to Ruth's specification.

▲ These silvery plants are perfect for rooftops. They are naturally from hot Mediterranean countries where the sun shines strongly and water is scarce – just like it may be on a roof garden. Their leaves are silvery to prevent water loss.

▲ The boundaries of the terrace have been formed by toughened glass held between steel uprights. They allow light to come into the garden and the occupants to see out.

▼ The room at the far end of the garden is perfect for outside eating.

▶ By using abundant planting in large containers, Ruth has given a very verdant, lush feel to the rooftop.

Terraces

With little space to work with, Amir Schlezinger from MyLandscapes has focused on making huge planters works of art, using a single piece of sculpture to finish off the space.

It's worth thinking about this option if your terrace is little more than a corridor – focus on what can be seen from inside the house and make the terrace work as a set piece.

Before

Planters with elegant strong lines are all that is needed to dress the terrace, but make sure the planters are big enough. If they aren't, the terrace will look half-hearted and half-finished.

These planters are made from powder-coated steel and as there was no access to the roof they had to be hauled up by crane.

Huge planters like this can be made from fibreglass and a local fabricator would be able to advise you on what designs would be possible – generally speaking containers made from flat planes of fibreglass like these are relatively easy to make and can be finished in a huge range of paint colours. By having them made to fit your space exactly the terrace probably won't need anything else, so it may prove a sound investment. Lit from behind they will look like works of art.

They can be made metres long and very deep. Filled with soil they would be incredibly heavy so either put in a false base for the soil or fill most of the space with perlite or something else bulky but light.

Garden Plan

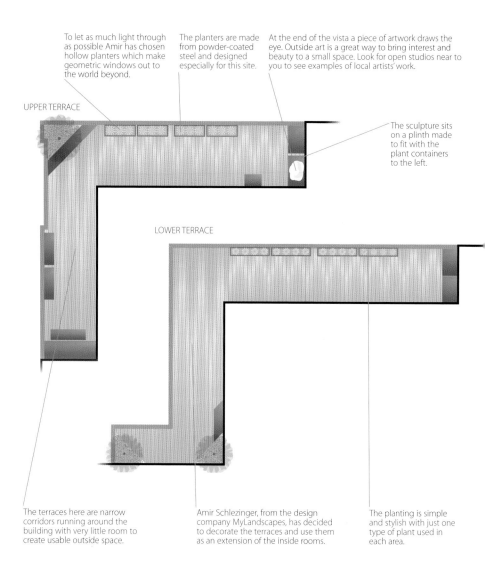

To let as much light through as possible Amir has chosen hollow planters which make geometric windows out to the world beyond.

The planters are made from powder-coated steel and designed especially for this site.

At the end of the vista a piece of artwork draws the eye. Outside art is a great way to bring interest and beauty to a small space. Look for open studios near to you to see examples of local artists' work.

UPPER TERRACE

The sculpture sits on a plinth made to fit with the plant containers to the left.

LOWER TERRACE

The terraces here are narrow corridors running around the building with very little room to create usable outside space.

Amir Schlezinger, from the design company MyLandscapes, has decided to decorate the terraces and use them as an extension of the inside rooms.

The planting is simple and stylish with just one type of plant used in each area.

▶ One of the wonderful things about this garden is its view of St Paul's Cathedral. Amir has placed a tree in the corner of the lower terrace to draw the eye and frame the view of the cathedral.

▲ On the lower terrace huge planters have been used again. Against a solid wall they don't need to let light through but their unique interlocking design makes a bold, sculptural statement.

◀ The lower terrace is visible from the higher one so it has to work when viewed from above.

▼ Polished stone paddles, laid on end, finish off this container perfectly.

▶ Low planters are used next to the wall of the sitting room.

Themed

This garden hangs off the side of a hillside where a flat area has been created outside the house before the land slopes away again. To hold the hillside up, there's an enormous wall along one side of the garden with brick buttresses jutting out at intervals. Not the most promising place to create a garden.

Garden designer Catherine Thomas was given a strong brief from the owners – they wanted a Mediterranean terrace. Catherine has used the potentially difficult terrain to make a wonderful garden. The wall has been rendered to make it brighter and lighter. By keeping the surface of the render quite rough and painting it an ochre colour it really helps to set the style for the garden. She has used the wall to create sheltered areas for planting and for two great features.

Near to the house she has included a long wall fountain which uses the height of the wall behind it to hold spouts reminiscent of a town fountain in Spain. The centrepiece to the whole garden is a raised in-built seat surrounded by terracotta tiles that uses the wall as its backdrop.

No grass was included, it would have meant importing top soil and in many ways a lawn is too English for this garden; the whole look evokes hot summers and baking sun, so gravel with its light-reflective qualities is perfect for the ground.

With its strong style the whole garden looks wonderfully complete, each object fits with the theme and adds to the look.

Garden Plan

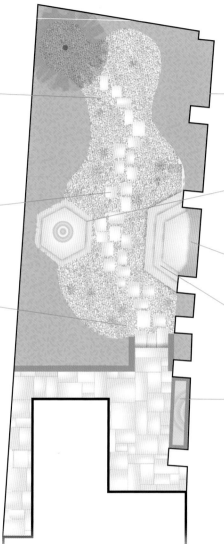

Gravel on the ground helps to continue the dry, bright, Mediterranean look. Plants are placed in the gravel, with pockets of good soil to grow in.

The garden is hugging the side of a hill – with a huge retaining wall on one side and views out on the other.

The owners wanted a Mediterranean feel to the terrace: the render on the walls, mixed with brick, gives this look.

To give definition to the garden, millstone flags from Stonemarket have been used to mark pathways.

The raised seat not only looks good but also gives the best views out from the garden.

It's also achieved by using terracotta tiles on the floors and for the in-built seat.

Ornaments and terracotta pots, often filled with bright red geraniums, also give this garden a real Mediterranean feel.

With the side wall such a dominant feature, the garden has to incorporate and use this height. The garden designer, Catherine Thomas, has used the wall to make raised sitting areas and a raised pool.

▶ A large urn has been turned into a water feature. The water falls over the side of the urn to an underground reservoir, hidden under the cobbles and under a grate. To make the feature look right Catherine has used terracotta tiles to surround it and frame it.

▲ Underneath the seat is a line of bright blue mosaic tiles.

▲ Many of the plants are evergreen so, even in the winter, there is plenty to see.

▲ Large containers make a bolder statement and can hold larger plants, but again, they've been grouped together to give an informal look.

◀ Bright red geraniums in pots on the walls could have come straight from southern France or Spain.

▼ The wall, with its enormous brick buttresses, has been used to house this inviting seating area. The warm coloured wall, the terracotta tiles, the plants and the accessories all add to the Mediterranean inspired effect.

▲ There's no grass in this garden but plenty of greenery and softness. The soil here is mostly of rubble – no good for lawn, but well suited to the needs of Mediterranean plants.

◄ It's amazing how a rendered wall can be changed so much by what's along its top, the capping. No capping at all and it looks smooth, sleek and modern. The same wall, the same render, but with bricks along the top, looks like it comes from a Spanish country garden.

▶ Tucked away in a corner is a small metal table and chairs.

Jacuzzi

This garden naturally leant itself to being divided into different areas. There are storage places and air vents running across it which couldn't be moved or changed, but they naturally divided the garden into three parts. Rather than fight against this, the design uses it as a starting point to organise the garden.

To one side is an area of quiet relaxation, a Zen garden with gravel and a freestanding hammock with views out across London. Shaped gravel on the ground is reminiscent of a Japanese contemplative space.

In the centre is a spa garden with a Jacuzzi, again it's all on the side with great views across the Thames. Clear glass is used for the screening – to keep out the wind without spoiling the view.

And to the other side is the area for entertaining, with low chairs and tables.

All around structural evergreen planting has been used to reinforce these divisions. Bamboo and box balls stay green through winter and require little maintenance. The oriental theme has been carried through the garden in the sculptures used.

And at night the garden takes on a magical air with coloured lights, exciting and bright enough to hold their own against the backdrop of the city.

Garden Plan

The hammock is freestanding and fits with the ambience of the Japanese-style garden.

This rooftop in central London has been divided up into different areas. This, the relaxation area has a hammock and a Zen garden.

In the gravel, garden driftwood sculpture and stones have been placed on 'plinths' of marked circles in the gravel.

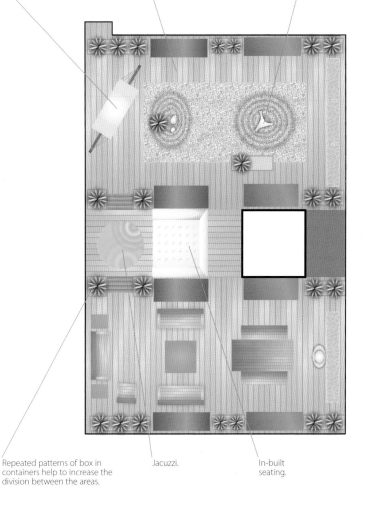

Repeated patterns of box in containers help to increase the division between the areas.

Jacuzzi.

In-built seating.

▷ Bamboo gives an evergreen screen to the sides, where the view is not so good.

▲ If you want a Jacuzzi on a roof and want to be able to see out, a Perspex screen around will keep out the cold wind.

▼ The garden has had to fit around the building's exterior structure and the designers have used the vents to divide up the different areas.

▷ The oriental theme has been carried through to the sculptures and statuary.

◀ The hammock has the best view in the garden, overlooking the river. Its sculptural shape adds to the Japanese feeling of the garden.

▲ This is a roof garden where the views out are everything. So the designers have put very few tall things in to block the panorama.

▼ The spiral of pebbles can be changed by the owner, to make new shapes.

Hillside

This garden was a steep slope dropping away from the house which was overgrown and unusable. Terracing was needed to create places to sit and enjoy the garden.

Before

Rather than making large terraces, Debbie Roberts, from design company Acres Wild, has made terraces going across the garden and descending the slope. These form intimate rooms, each with its own view out down the garden. The shapes of the rooms have been reinforced by beautifully made, in-built wooden benches. This is a great advertisement for very bold lines and shapes in a design. All through the year the forms of the decks and the strong line of the lower retaining wall maintain the garden's architecture, and in the summer, these lines remain but are softened by abundant planting.

A huge factor in the design of this garden was the maintenance. The garden is large so, in order to keep it manageable, the planting has been carefully thought out. A strong structure of evergreens has been planted. Tall bamboos and shrubs make the backdrop and around the terraces are hebes, yews, spiky New Zealand flax and palms. These all take very little maintenance. On top of this are the pretties. To keep the maintenance of these down, a very limited palette has been used and the daylilies, purple-top verbena and red hot pokers have been planted in swathes through the garden. The idea is that these will need to be cut back – but only once a year – and as the owners will be able to use shears rather than secateurs the job will be done very quickly.

Garden Plan

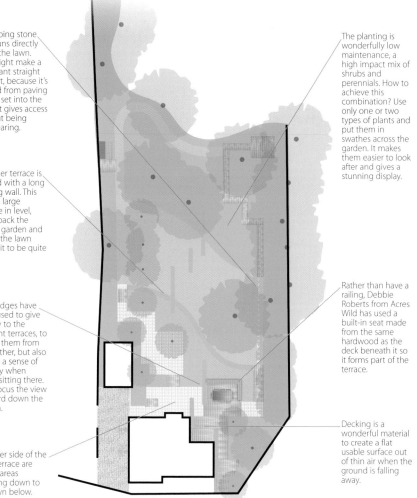

A stepping stone path runs directly down the lawn. This might make a dominant straight line but, because it's formed from paving stones set into the grass, it gives access without being overbearing.

A further terrace is formed with a long curving wall. This takes a large change in level, holds back the higher garden and allows the lawn below it to be quite level.

Box hedges have been used to give privacy to the different terraces, to screen them from each other, but also to give a sense of security when you're sitting there. They focus the view outward down the garden.

To either side of the deck terrace are paved areas stepping down to the lawn below.

The planting is wonderfully low maintenance, a high impact mix of shrubs and perennials. How to achieve this combination? Use only one or two types of plants and put them in swathes across the garden. It makes them easier to look after and gives a stunning display.

Rather than have a railing, Debbie Roberts from Acres Wild has used a built-in seat made from the same hardwood as the deck beneath it so it forms part of the terrace.

Decking is a wonderful material to create a flat usable surface out of thin air when the ground is falling away.

▶ Debbie has used quite tall trees to give height to the planting; these are standards with clear stems up to five feet so they don't impede the view when you're sitting on the terrace.

▲ Giant feather grass and purple-top verbena (verbena bonariensis) make a perfect combination to catch the setting sun. They grow to about five feet tall and will form a transparent barrier in the summer time.

◄ The built-in benches have been made from hardwood.

▲ High-impact planting like this looks great and is also easier to maintain than a hodgepodge of different plants. A line of low grasses at the front, then a line of ferns, and backed by some evergreen shrubs. They will need a once-a-year trim back in early spring.

▼ Alongside the retaining wall Debbie has planted a line of daylilies which look magnificent throughout the summer. The wall itself gives structure in the winter and at its end is an evergreen hebe which adds a touch of green all year round.

▲ At the top of the steps down to the main lawn is a seat which enjoys the view right down the garden.

▼ The terraces have been formed into separate rooms. They catch the sun at different times of the day and, to get more of a feeling of separation, they have different materials on the floor.

▷ With no time or space for a vegetable garden the owners grow their vegetables in pots on the terraces.

Minimalist

If space and time are limited it's always a good idea to consider a beautifully minimalist approach to the design of a roof or terrace. Here there is only a narrow corridor between two buildings – a space which rarely gets the sun and is overlooked from above.

Before

The owners wanted a low-maintenance usable space which fitted with the high standards of their apartment inside the building. They appreciated they might not use the space a great deal but it had to make a beautiful view from inside the property.

Urban Roof Gardens, the designers of the garden, have created a minimalist space and used the best materials finished to the highest standards. Planting has been kept to a minimum with wonderful stainless-steel planters filled with low-maintenance plants.

A seating area has been allowed for near the door, and a sun sail to protect it from hot overhead sun has been included in the design.

9

Garden Plan

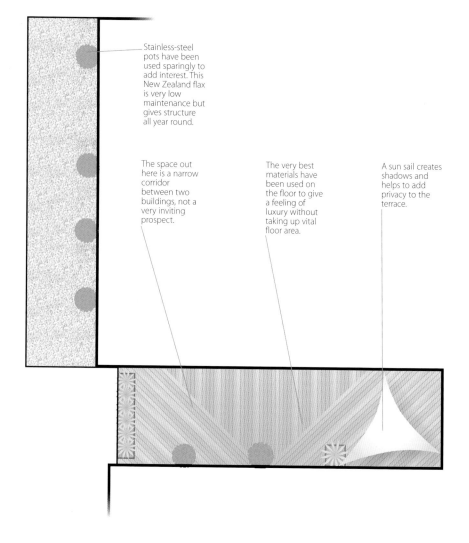

Stainless-steel pots have been used sparingly to add interest. This New Zealand flax is very low maintenance but gives structure all year round.

The space out here is a narrow corridor between two buildings, not a very inviting prospect.

The very best materials have been used on the floor to give a feeling of luxury without taking up vital floor area.

A sun sail creates shadows and helps to add privacy to the terrace.

▶ Rather than laying the decking straight across or down the space it has been laid on diagonals to give a feeling of movement to the space.

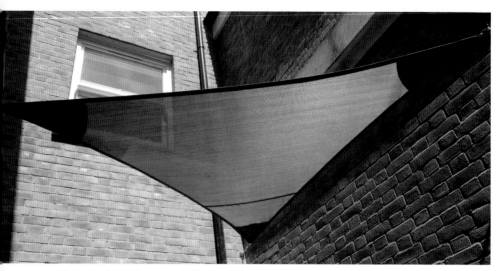

▲ The sun sail provides some shelter and privacy without jumping out or cutting out too much light.

▼ The materials are of a very high quality and the level of detailing is good. A hardwood, ipe, gives a red-brown effect

▶ Even where it's too dangerous for people to walk, there is room for a repeated pattern of containers and trees in the gaps between windows to make the view from the street better.

◀ The red in the leaves of the New Zealand flax picks up the reds in the wood and contrasts with the silver of the containers.

▲ Something that's rarely mentioned about decking especially good quality, hard wood decking it looks wonderful when it's wet.

▼ The stainless-steel containers help to provide privacy from the street below.

Desert style

If you think this design looks simple it's doing its job very well. It is a minimalist design but a great deal of thought has gone into making some very difficult areas work well.

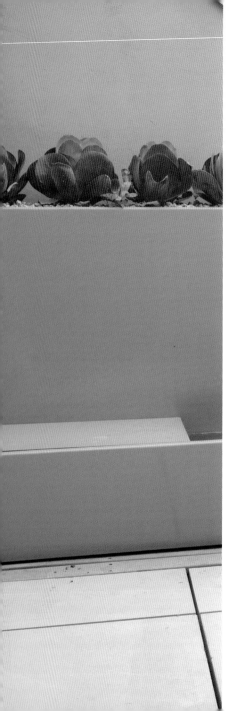

There are two distinct terraces here. The south-facing one has a desert theme: century plants, sandstone-coloured walls and the waterfall all go with the hot sunny aspect. The north-facing terrace is more shady and has a bar and seating. The landscape designer, Amir Schlezinger from the design company MyLandscapes, has transformed these narrow corridors into distinct, usable and beautiful spaces.

On the south side there is an inviting outside sitting room complete with sofa and carpet and an overhead canopy to reinforce the ambiguity of inside/outside.

However, the real reason this garden works is the way the design is hard-wired into the space. The garden designer didn't come along here at the last minute to make the most of what was available, he was able to put in walls to suit the design with niches for artwork and voids for water features. Even the height of the perimeter walls has been designed in to fit with the different sitting areas. This is a great advertisement for getting a garden designer involved at the earliest stages of the process of creating a roof terrace.

Garden Plan

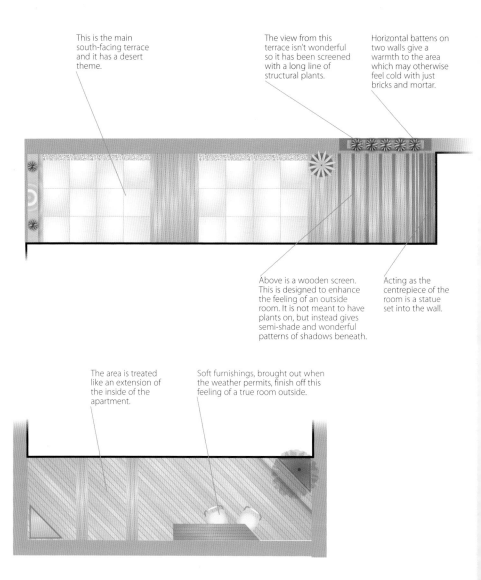

This is the main south-facing terrace and it has a desert theme.

The view from this terrace isn't wonderful so it has been screened with a long line of structural plants.

Horizontal battens on two walls give a warmth to the area which may otherwise feel cold with just bricks and mortar.

Above is a wooden screen. This is designed to enhance the feeling of an outside room. It is not meant to have plants on, but instead gives semi-shade and wonderful patterns of shadows beneath.

Acting as the centrepiece of the room is a statue set into the wall.

The area is treated like an extension of the inside of the apartment.

Soft furnishings, brought out when the weather permits, finish off this feeling of a true room outside.

The doors of the apartment open up so the outside is a real extension of the living space.

⚠ A niche has been created in the far wall of the garden for art and sculpture.

◁ At night the lighting on the terrace is stunning. Two lights are used here – a downlighter under the seat and an uplighter to catch the leaves of the tree.

⚠ Tender plants which can be changed with the seasons and with your mood are used in many of the pots. These containers have been dressed with silver-coloured gravel to complement the silvery leaves above and the silver containers below.

▽ On the north-facing terrace is a breakfast bar, with views out across the rooftops. A rug is used to give a homely feel to this outside space.

▲ Any table, built-in seat or overhang can be lit from below and will, most likely, give a wonderful effect. The light source is hidden and the surface above appears to float.

▼ There is something really special about having a sofa and proper cushions outside. If you can work out a way to have these outside but have storage so they can be easily brought in, you will find yourself spending more time outdoors, simply because it's more comfortable to sit out.

▶ Amir has used a limited palette of plants to give accents throughout the garden. This, and the same colour of paint on the walls, unifies the spaces.

Directory

Products

AHS Direct
Garden and home
www.ahsdirect.co.uk

Alan Wilson
Contemporary water features and sculpture
www.thesculptureworkshop.co.uk

Balcony Systems Ltd
Specialists in sophisticated balustrading and glazing solutions
www.balconette.co.uk

Blackdown Horticultural Consultants
Green roof specialists
www.greenroof.co.uk

Cheeky Mojito
Outdoor art canvasses
www.cheekymojito.com

Coolscapes
Water sculpture
www.coolscapes.co.uk

David Harber
Sundials, sculpture and water features for the garden
www.davidharber.com

Foxes Boxes
Creative window box and balcony dressing
www.foxesboxes.co.uk

ingarden
Products for modern outdoor living
www.ingarden.co.uk

Insideout Garden Art
Weatherproof images to decorate your outdoor space
www.insideout-gardenart.co.uk

John Cullen Lighting
Lighting design and supply for inside and outside the home
www.johncullenlighting.co.uk

LazyLawn™
Natural looking artificial grass
www.evergreensuk.com

Moussem Tents
Moroccan tents
www.moussemtents.co.uk

Raw Garden
Modern outdoor equipment
www.rawgarden.co.uk

Stonemarket
Garden landscape products
www.stonemarket.co.uk

Susan Bradley
Objects and furniture
www.susanbradley.co.uk

The Garden Trellis Company
Trellis and garden woodwork
www.gardentrellis.co.uk

Urban Roof Gardens
Creation and design of modern roof gardens
www.urbanroofgardens.com

Urbis Design
Modern curvy planters
www.urbisdesign.co.uk

Designers

Acres Wild Garden and Landscape Design
www.acreswild.co.uk

Amir Schlezinger
MyLandscapes roof terraces and gardens
www.mylandscapes.co.uk

Catherine Thomas Landscape and Garden Design
www.catherinethomas.co.uk

Charlotte Rowe Garden Design
www.charlotterowe.com

Emma Plunket
www.plunketgardens.com

Pamela Johnson Garden Design
www.pamelajohnson.co.uk

Ruth Marshall
Cool Gardens Landscaping
www.coolgardens.co.uk

Sara Jane Rothwell
Glorious Gardens
www.gloriousgardendesign.co.uk

Site Specific Ltd
Interior design and more
www.sitespecificltd.co.uk

Urban Roof Gardens
www.urbanroofgardens.com